The Shell Book of
Cottages

The Shell Book of
Cottages

Richard Reid

MICHAEL JOSEPH

Published in Great Britain by Michael Joseph Ltd
52 Bedford Square London WC1B 3EF

ISBN 0 7181 1630 5

This book was designed and produced by George Rainbird Ltd
36 Park Street, London W1Y 4DE

House Editor: Georgina Dowse
Designer: Christopher Sorrell
Cartographer: Tom Stalker Miller
Indexer: Penelope Miller

Printed and bound in Great Britain by Jarrold & Sons Ltd,
Norwich, Norfolk

The pictures on the jacket: (front) Cottages at
Buckland-in-the-Moor, Devon
(back) Gold Hill, Shaftesbury, Dorset

The picture on the title page:
Tudor cottage at Cerne Abbas, Dorset

To Thalia

Contents

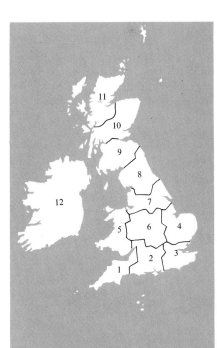

Author's Acknowledgments

For those interested in cottage building this is very much a beginner's book, and I am a beginner. My interest in, and subsequent study of, the traditional building of the British Isles was stimulated by the work and lectures of Ronald Brunskill. Most writers in this field owe much to his work, I more than any. And, of course, there are others, many others, whose scholarship over numerous years make books like mine possible. There is a complete bibliography at the end of this book, but I do owe a particular debt to the work of M. W. Barley's two books, *The English Farmhouse and Cottage* and *The House and Home*. Professor Barley has allowed me to adapt a number of the drawings in his books for the purpose of this book of mine. I also acknowledge my debt to writing and drawings in Eric Mercer's *English Vernacular Houses* and Peter Smith's *Houses of the Welsh Countryside* and in books by Alec Clifton-Taylor, Gillian Darley, Estyn Evans, Colin Sinclair, Caoimhín Ó Danachair, A. Gailey, and F. H. A. Aalen; and to the Royal Commission on Historical Monuments and Her Majesty's Stationery Office.

I am most grateful to Philip Jaques of Shell and John Hadfield of Rainbirds for giving me the opportunity to write this book; to Georgina Dowse, my editor, for making sense of my non-sense; to Denis Bosdet of Linden Artists, my agents; and finally to my family for patiently putting up with my absence from numerous family gatherings or fireside evenings as I worked on the book.

EDITORIAL NOTES

The following abbreviations have been used in the line drawings: B = bedroom, Bd = bed, Bn = barn, Bt = buttery, By = byre, C = closet, D = dairy, E = entrance, F = fire, H = hall, Hs = house, K = kitchen, P = porch, Pa = parlour, R = room, S = store, Sc = scullery, Sh = shippon, St = stable. Inevitably technical terms have been used in the text and a glossary explaining these will be found at the end of the book.

MAPS

A map of Great Britain and Ireland will be found on page 7 showing how the book is divided into regions. There is also a map on page 25 illustrating regional characteristics and the distribution of building materials and methods. A map will be found at the beginning of each regional section showing the new county and regional boundaries in Great Britain and also the places mentioned in the text.

Introduction

Today, the cottage, small, often pretty and usually cosy, represents something totally different from its original, the shanty built at night on the village wastelands of medieval England. Both the cottage, and its original, the shanty, are still found. All that has changed is their context and, with that, their circumstances. To the Tudor gentleman housed in his elegant manor, the cottage must have seemed a fairly destitute affair. Today his equivalent is probably happily housed in a modernized version of that same cottage deep in the heart of the stockbroker belt – and there are many who will think him lucky. We must look further afield for our equivalent of the medieval shanty. It is found in the slums between the big city airport and big city hotel in the developing world. We can imagine the scene today: smoke from cooking pots in backyards, mile upon mile of little alleyways snaking through densely-packed huts of straw, crumbling brick or beaten tin cans. The worst is usually hidden away near the city centre – dense, filthy tenements which are usually the first staging port for rural migrants. The problem of unemployment reappears bringing with it all the miseries of overcrowding, decaying houses, filth, noise, and an altogether alien and hostile environment. This is the urban crisis in the underdeveloped world in the twentieth century and, as a precautionary tale shows, it could be ours tomorrow.

In *Billenium* J. G. Ballard describes the horrors of an overcrowded city of the future with families living in staircase cubicles while the streets were so crowded that vehicular traffic had ceased, and pedestrian jams occurred. The outward growth of cities had by then been checked. All over the world the former suburban areas were being reclaimed for agriculture while increased population was confined to the urban ghettos. The countryside as such, no longer existed. Every single square foot of ground sprouted a crop of one type or other. The one-time fields and meadows of the world were now, in effect, factory floors, as highly mechanized and closed to the public as any industrial area.

The cottage today represents that other dream, Virgil's myth of a Golden Age in which man lived on the fruits of the earth, peacefully, piously and with primitive simplicity. Claude, the painter, depicted such a world with his pictures of grazing sheep, unruffled waters and calm skies; images of perfect harmony between man and nature. But these are painted as if he knew the perfection could last no longer than the moment in which it takes possession of our minds. Today, the loving care that many lavish on their country cottages is, in their own way, an attempt to colonize, or perhaps to recolonize, such a Golden Age, by shutting outside that other world, a technological world, hedonistic, cynical and insensitive. But is their dream possible? Is it really to be found deep in the hop fields of the Kentish Weald, in the hilly countryside of the Cotswolds, or snug in the valleys of Wales? Perhaps it can be no more than a breath of air, a fleeting moment of perfection no longer than a weekend break. But in the attempt

11

The Hay Wain, *by John Constable, 1821. This
is the epitome of the nineteenth-century
Virgilian scene.*

to track down this dream the landscape of Britain and Ireland has become re-colonized.

In Neolithic times the population of Britain was little more than 20,000 which is the size today of an average country town. A basic existence was scratched from pasture farming. By the Iron Age (from 500 B.C. to the coming of the Romans at the beginning of the first century A.D.) development in agriculture led to the appearance of numerous villages, many of them little different in appearance from reconstructions of Glastonbury Lake Village. With the spread of settled villages the population in Britain rose to something in the region of a quarter of a million. On the eve of the

A hut typical of the Iron Age (500 B.C. to the Roman invasion) is seen in the reconstruction of Glastonbury Lake Village, Somerset.

Roman Conquest it was probably a little over 400,000. The Romans brought improved methods of agriculture, the construction of roads and bridges, the building of country villas and the development of towns. The population by this time had increased to 700,000. The Romans cleared and farmed the landscape, drained the Fens and created rich farmland. As the Anglo-Saxons gradually took over following the departure of the Romans, much of the land was neglected. The Anglo-Saxon colonists slowly cut back the weeds and scrubs and salvaged building materials from the Roman ruins, but most of Britain was still virgin country. By 1066, however, England had become a land of villages. Gradually the woodlands of Anglo-Saxon England were reduced as small denes were cleared and cattle brought in to graze. Many of the early villages were built from huts erected by squatters on common pasture or in a clearing in thickly-wooded country. The Domesday Book records a population of approximately $1\frac{1}{4}$ million with East Anglia being the most densely populated while Yorkshire had less than 30,000 people at this time.

After the Norman Conquest England was divided into 'manors'. The wealthier Norman landowners possessed several manors. Although such a landlord would probably have his own castle, he would invariably spend time in each of his manors and he therefore built himself a manor house in each one. Most of the servants were quartered in the Great House, but for the farm labourers connected with the manor, simple cottages were built nearby.

Before the fifteenth century England must have appeared like an unending forest. Gradually the wild hillsides were being cultivated and the land now was richer than it had been during Roman times. By the coming of the Black Death in 1348 the population of England had reached $3\frac{3}{4}$ million. Towns were now a common feature in the rural landscape of medieval England.

Great changes occurred following the Black Death. Over one-third of the population had died. Labour shortages increased the cost of labour. Under feudalism serfs worked forty days a year on the lord's land without payment. Now pressure increased for the lord to commute the services for a money wage, thus making the serf a freeman. Many of the villages that had been depopulated by the plague remained deserted. Others were gradually abandoned partly because landlords were unable to maintain the traditional animal husbandry without the necessary labour. They switched to pastoral farming which needed only a fraction of the labour. Where the landlord owned most of the land, he evicted the remaining peasants, demolished the village houses and converted the open arable fields into large enclosures of pasture for cattle and sheep. The evicted labourer, now landless, moved into a neighbouring village to live with relatives or friends or to build a shanty on the village wasteland.

It is here that the story of the cottage really begins – in the Middle Ages. The cottage then was seldom more than a rough shanty, built from the ground, either of wattle and daub or mud, and roofed with a thatching of straw or reed or turves of growing grass or moss. These buildings were so fragile that any violent storm could destroy them. A thief would debate whether to force the door or break down the wall.

Towards the close of the fourteenth century these shanties were gradually replaced by the more permanent cruck-framed buildings that are still found in the twentieth century.

But, of course, the history of the cottage is really a history of the poor, the wholesale robbery of the land for enclosures, the Industrial Revolution, and the making of the British working class.

The Tudor mansion was matched by the yeoman's new farmhouse and by the labourer's cottage planted at night on the common. By the nineteenth century the common land had been enclosed, the freehold farmer was left to go bankrupt and the industrial worker had to accept what housing the mine and mill owner provided for him. The concentration of property into fewer hands, the denial of opportunity and the subsequent pattern of dependence it created was a condition that was unacceptable to the liberal. But there was little he could do about it.

Today it is the cottage itself that is changing hands. Just as the nineteenth-century countryman escaped to the towns of the industrial north for much needed work, so the twentieth-century townsman escapes from his work to a cottage hideaway in some rural retreat.

History

The earliest traditional houses were dwellings of one, two or occasionally three rooms, with low walls and a low roof above. The walls were built of earth, thin timbers, turf, chalk or stone. These houses were often without chimneys or windows. A bonfire on the bare earth floor provided heat, the smoke filtering out through holes in the roof or walls. Such houses were built from the Dark Ages onwards, but usually they were so flimsy that, every generation or so, a new house was built on the same site.

In Elizabethan times the nouveau riche built their mansions and the new yeoman class, prosperous from the wool trade, built farmhouses. But while wool made the yeoman rich it reduced the need for farm labour. The labourers became destitute and had no option but to become squatters. In the sixteenth century a man could build a house on

Neolithic Man (3000–1800 B.C.) adapted the primitive branch and thatch tents of the Mesolithic age by creating more headroom for himself by sinking his hut floor in a pit in the ground. These huts were usually circular in plan with a central pole to support the roof. In the Bronze Age (1800–500 B.C.) man built himself more substantial dwellings. Where stone was in abundance he built these more elaborate beehive huts of dry-stone walls. The stone roof was usually covered with a thatch of bracken and turf.

Beehive huts, Lewis, Scotland

Beehive huts, Ireland

Black house, Lewis, Scotland. These are found in the crofting communities of the Scottish islands. Those still inhabited now have chimneys and fireplaces, but originally the fireplace was in the middle of the floor, the smoke vented through a hole in the roof. Byre and living room are under the same roof.

15

common land if he could raise the roof over his head and have a fire burning in his grate between sunset and sunrise. These houses were built of mud and sticks. But in 1589 the Cottage Acts of Queen Elizabeth I were passed stating that in future no cottage was to be built unless four acres of land went with it.

While the Tudor élite tended towards violence and a lack of respect for the law, the lower ranks of rural society were still held together by a medieval respect for craftsmanship and established ways of working in a close-knit community.

Any improvement in housing standards took time to reach less populated areas. The sunken one-roomed dwellings recorded in Somerset in the 1880s or the cottages of turf or dry-stone walling common in Northumberland and the West Riding in the nineteenth century are no improvement on the Cornish husbandman's earth-walled, thatch-roofed house of the early sixteenth century. One major improvement from the Saxon hut to the Stuart cottage was not in the size, but in having walls of a man's height

Wealden house, Harrietsham, Kent. It was built in the late fifteenth century.

Late fifteenth-century hall house, Chiddingstone, Kent. It is built of close studding with a middle rail. The brick wall was added in the eighteenth century.

Cruck-built open hall house of the late fifteenth century, found today mainly along the northern stretches of the Hampshire-Surrey border or in parts of the South Midlands. They are smaller than the open hall houses of the southeast.

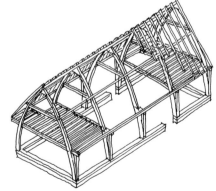

which meant that the floor no longer had to be sunk below ground level.

Cottages of this sort were built later in two very different ways. One way was to build better versions of the old houses, more spacious and of stouter materials. The second and more significant way was to build lofty open halls adapted from upper-class homes. Lofts began to appear in the early sixteenth century and by the late sixteenth century the two-storeyed house was standard throughout the southeast. These houses usually had three rooms but in Devon, Cornwall and Somerset the one-roomed house was still being built and it was not until the late sixteenth century that the two-roomed house was developed in western and southern England.

The lavatory, confined to the Great House, was, as in medieval times, still an upstairs closet with a stone or wooden seat over a chute. In the seventeenth century this was replaced by the commode but it was rare for the cottager to have one.

In the eighteenth century the rural labourers lived in a one-roomed cottage, sometimes with a lean-to shed, or out-shut. But generally they were better off than their European counterpart. They ate meat once or twice a week, supplied their own bacon and eggs and made their bread from rye or bran. By the 1740s rural life had begun to change rapidly. The wealthier landowners had already started enclosing their estates, evicting tenants and destroying their homes. This process, which created the hedgerows of the typical English countryside, was accelerated by the Parliamentary Enclosure Acts of 1761–1845.

Evicted farmers began to establish themselves on the less fertile moors, hills and mountains while the landless labourer began weaving, spinning, basket-

Some seventeenth-century houses in parts of Lincolnshire, Nottinghamshire, Lancashire and North Yorkshire had low lofts used for storage. Many of these houses were built of mud and stud.

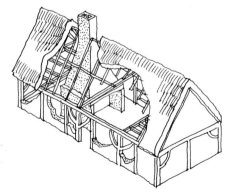

Two-storey cottage in the southeast, showing jettied timber work, typical of fifteenth- and sixteenth-century houses. The whole of the oak frame was tenoned and pinned together. Various methods and materials were used to fill in the panels between the studs. The most common practice was wattle and daub or brick nogging.

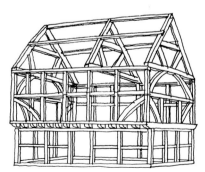

Cottage, Rempstone, Nottinghamshire. Built of timber in the seventeenth century, it consists of three cells of one storey with a loft above.

Church cottage, Swindon, Wiltshire. Built in 1700 it consists of one storey with two cells and an attic above.

making and other home crafts to earn a little extra.

Bad harvests in the 1760s and 1770s and the wars with France forced prices up but wages were not increased. Under the Act of Settlement of 1662 anyone was eligible for some kind of relief from the parish where he was born or had settled in. But many landowners, in order to reduce their liability for poor rate, let cottages decay and, in some cases, pulled them down. By doing this they could also force so-called undesirables to move.

In the late eighteenth century some liberals, appalled by conditions for many cottagers, began to raise questions. An agriculturist and land valuer named Nathaniel Kent pointed out in his book *Hints to Gentlemen of Landed Property* (1775) the absurdity of landlords providing elaborate stables and kennels while neglecting the cottages, for it was the cottagers who would provide the hands to cultivate the land. Kent's book was the first to contain plans for model cottages. John Wood, the designer of the Royal Crescent in Bath, produced an architectural book in 1781 devoted entirely to cottages insisting, among other things, on

regularity, which to him constituted beauty. By the late eighteenth century some landlords saw cottage building simply as an artistic exercise. After 1780 designs for cottages began to appear in architectural pattern books. The emphasis moved away from Wood's more classical stance to a celebration of the purely rustic and picturesque.

James Molton in his *Essay on British Cottage Architecture* (1798) suggested an irregularity in colour, texture and materials sufficient to produce an effect of accident. Others tried to create the effect of a painting. In *Sketches in Architecture* (1798) Sir John Soane included designs for cottages combining rusticity with the regularity of antiquity. The villages of Blaise near Bath, and Milton Abbas in Dorset, are very much influenced by his sketches but it was a minority who built picturesquely; most built the purely utilitarian.

The vast increase in cotton from the cotton mills in the 1770s led to the amazing expansion of weaving throughout southeast Lancashire. It was the loom and not the cotton mill which attracted immigrants in their thousands and small

Many cottages built by landlords were often very primitive in comparison to the stables they built for their animals.

farmers and agricultural labourers entered the trade and became weavers. The old loom shops could not cope, so new weavers' cottages with loom shops rose up in every direction. The golden age of the trade was between 1788 and 1803.

Between 1790 and 1810 it was a matter of policy to increase the dependence of reserves of cheap labour for the convenience of the farmer at haymaking and harvest, for roadmaking and fencing. Some gentry, particularly in the north, saw the French wars as a means of reducing wages, with higher prices and fewer jobs. Overpopulation of the commons by cottagers and squatters antagonized the small proprietor, while panic

and the class struggle inflamed in the aristocracy by the French Revolution led to greater exploitation by master of servant. The wars suppressed both urban reformers and the more humane gentry. A new argument was added to the arguments of greed, that of social discipline, and the commons were now seen as dangerous centres of indiscipline.

The ending of the French wars in 1815 created widespread unemployment. The village population was enlarged by soldiers returning from the wars; labourers were joined by bankrupt smallholders. The northern and Midlands' textile industry flourished, weakening the position of labourers elsewhere. As domestic

19

employment slackened, the cheap labour of women for agriculture grew. Refugees from the country fled to the blast furnaces, cotton mills and coal mines of the new industrial north. The wool industry was slowly transformed. Power spinning was driving out hand spinning, but the weaving factories were not yet established on a large scale. The French wars had brought a boom to the iron, coal and engineering industries and the railway age, beginning in the 1830s, transformed them into the major source of national wealth. Before the Battle of Waterloo (1815) the network of canals was almost complete but McAdam and Telford were remaking the roads during this period.

But for many people the village was still the main focus of life. Enclosures of the open fields had made agriculture more efficient, but much of the land was now in the hands of wealthy men who let it to tenant farmers. Many smallholders had become landless agricultural labourers or had fled to the new towns. The corn laws and the game laws strangled the poor.

Southern landowners attacked the right of poor relief for its apparent encouragement of the idleness and depravity of the working class. The young and single had some future, but the mature labourer with a family was in danger of losing his last inheritance – the poor rate. The gentry was using cheap labour gangs, humiliating labour auctions, and men were harnessed in carts. Many felt it was preferable to be slaves at once than to work under such a system. Minor incidents led to the labourers' riots in southern England in 1830. The result was a temporary rise in wages. The middle classes were deeply shocked and supported the working classes in thought if not action. For the poor merely to have

a sound roof was considered a blessing. Mud cottages were still common as not everyone could afford more substantial materials. Redundant farmhouses in East Anglian villages were converted to cottages. In the north most unmarried labourers boarded in the farmhouses since housing the labourer was still considered of little importance. The more fortunate cottager with a garden could at least provide food for the table. But many lived in tied cottages, and all were subject to dismissal at any time.

Following the post-war depression farming began to prosper. In 1839 The Royal Agricultural Society was formed and the Society, together with some enlightened landowners, took a keen interest in the labourers' well-being. Some cottages built in the late nineteenth century even had earth closets, but conditions deteriorated after the disastrous harvest of 1879 and farm workers flocked to the towns in search of better living conditions and employment. The expansion of heavy industry during the era of the railways also helped turn the countryman into an urban industrial worker, sweating in the mines and mills where he was harnessed to machines. The new industrial towns built the future slums. The improvement of streets and buildings had been carried out with vigour after the passing of the Improvement Act of 1850. But the cellar rooms of Liverpool, the tenements of Glasgow and the back-to-back housing of the West Riding, which led to the industrial suburbs, like those outside Leeds, became more unhealthy than the city centres. There was a certain amount of working-class self-help through freehold land societies, while the mill owners and railway companies built houses to let. Disraeli's Artisans' Dwellings Act of 1875 provided for the compulsory acquisi-

*The old country cottages, like these, had a
rustic charm that became idealized in painting
and literature.*

tion by local authorities of insanitary areas. After acquiring such areas existing properties were demolished and new houses built. In 1884 a Royal Commission was set up to re-examine the special housing problems of the working classes.

Agriculture prospered with improved methods of stock breeding, draining and manufacturing, machine ploughing, reaping and threshing. A surplus of labour and higher prices combined with the gold discoveries of the fifties and the peace of the sixties lulled the Victorian capitalist into a complacent philanthropy. The first of the new model towns was begun at Saltaire. This was followed in the 1890s by Bournville, Port Sunlight, and the first of the garden cities.

The invention of the Hoffmann Kiln (1858), which mechanized brick production, and the development of cheap, speedy transport changed the dependence of houses and cottages on local materials. The uniformity of the Victorian red brick obliterated the distinctive character and colour of particular localities. Old and well-tried local craftsmanship gave way to mass-produced work assembled by semi-skilled labour.

During the 1890s the pull of London tightened. Local newspapers gave way to the nationals. Political and economic trends began to depend less on local forces and more on national pressures at the centre. And it was then, as the building bylaws of the 1875 Public Health Act took effect, that one began to see the same kind of working-class housing everywhere.

While the Victorians abolished slavery, raised the standard of medical care and reduced the distress of destitution, they created the drab squalor of mining and industrial cities, the ravages of the countryside and the menace of mass unemployment. In the early part of this century some farm labourers' wages were still at eighteenth-century levels. Many did not have fresh meat once a week, and many were still housed in cramped conditions.

With the building of garden cities such as Letchworth and Welwyn at the beginning of the twentieth century, architects were given the opportunity to experiment with practical, cheap, rural housing on a large scale. The worker was housed increasingly by the Council and his cottage passed into the hands of the professional and managerial class. Rooms were added, *bijou* decor replaced the austere, gardens became more ornamental and picturesque, and gradually the cottage became very much a house.

Regional Styles

The Great Houses were shaped primarily by taste and culture. Just as contact with the Crusaders had influenced the building of the Welsh border castles, so such contacts as Henry VIII made with Francis I on the Field of the Cloth of Gold (1520) brought the Renaissance to Britain and fashioned our later mansions. But for the artisan and labourer, size and type of accommodation and the availability of materials were the primary factors governing cottage building. Type of accommodation produced distinctive forms, like the Cumbrian longhouse or the weavers' cottages of Lancashire; materials gave them shape and style, as can be seen in the raised plasterwork (pargeting) of seventeenth-century Suffolk or the basic constructional systems of the timber cruck and box frame. With the exception of the Great House, it was rare, before the age of cheap transport, to see stone houses in low-lying marshy areas or in wooded regions. Similarly buildings of brick and unbaked earth were scarce on the limestone belt and on the granite uplands of the southwest.

The thirteenth-century forests, consisting mainly of hardwoods, were enormous. Wealden oak was famous and the Welsh border counties comprised one vast oak forest. Timber-framed structures evolved from cruck construction which used two curved tree trunks fixed at the top in the shape of a gable and spaced in bays and built on a plinth. Houses were usually of two or more bays their divisions being marked by crucks. These simple single-storey houses developed with the introduction of tie beams which allowed for the insertion of an intermediate floor. Cruck construction, found primarily in fifteenth-century Wales and in the north of England, was restricted in width and height according to the size of timbers available for the crucks. Such restrictions were resolved by the development of the box frame in the more sophisticated areas of southern and eastern England.

Primitive croft on the Isle of Skye. Note the rough thatch enclosing the chimney and weighted down by stones.

House built of stone at Low Hartsop, Patterdale, Cumbria in the late seventeenth century. Note the distinctive rounded chimneys.

Cruck-framed house

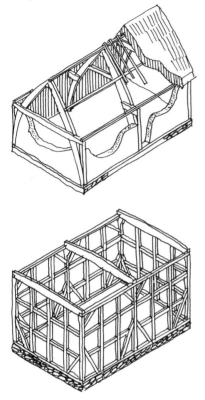

REGIONAL CHARACTERISTICS

 Sandstone

 Limestone

 Granite

Slate

△ Roofing

■ Walling

Box-framed house. The choice of walling material dictated the choice of structural system. The two options open to the builder were mass construction or frame construction. With mass construction (see page 26) the roof loads were carried to the foundations by the walls themselves. The wall was also the weather-protective envelope. With frame construction the loads are carried by only the frame itself; the infill panels, usually wattle and daub or brick nogging which act as the weather-protective envelope, are non-loadbearing. A characteristic of the southeast is the use of a cladding of plain tiles, mathematical tiles or weatherboarding to conceal the frame. And for the timber-built house there were two means of framing – cruck framing, associated more with medieval buildings, although there are examples well into the nineteenth century, and box-frame construction which has continued to the present day.

STONE △

CORBELS △

△ TURF

△ HEATHER
   THATCH

■ STONE
   RUBBLE
   WALLING

△ SLATE

△ STONE SLATES

PANTILES △

△ FURZE
   THATCH

△ SLATE

PANTILES △

PEBBLE ■

REED △
THATCH

■ STONE
   RUBBLE
   WALLING

■ TIMBER
   FRAME

STRAW
THATCH △

△ TIMBER
   FRAME

COTSWOLD STONE ■

PLAIN
TILES △

△ PANTILES

△ STONE SLATES

△ STONE
   SLATES

△ PLAIN
   TILES

■ BATH
   STONE

△ TIMBER
   FRAME

△ PANTILES

COB ■

△ STRAW THATCH

△ PLAIN
   TILES

△ HEATHER
   THATCH

△ STONE SLATES

The timbers used in these areas were of great size because of the abundance of oak in the early sixteenth century, but by the seventeenth century things had changed. Brick and stone carried more status for the wealthy but for the poor, however, timber was still used and there was a shortage of timber due to its prodigal use for iron smelting and shipbuilding. Timber framing was replaced by half-timbering which used smaller and fewer timbers with squarer infill panels. These panels were originally filled with wattle and daub but this was replaced later by brick nogging. During the late seventeenth century in Kent, Sussex and Surrey timber framing was covered by weatherboarding or by the distinctive patterns used in tile hanging. In the Georgian period the ingenious mathematical tile, seen best at Lewes in Sussex, was developed giving buildings a bricklike appearance but avoiding the brick taxes.

The juxtaposition of timber and stone

Mass construction

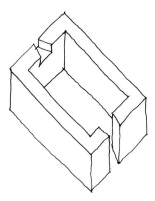

An early-nineteenth-century weatherboarded cottage in Sussex

Cottage of the Kentish yeoman type at Bignor, West Sussex. The house consists of a central hall flanked by storeyed ends with projecting upper floors. Originally the hall would be open to the roof. Good examples are to be found in Kent at Goudhurst and Shorne.

Decorative tile hanging, Chiddingstone, Kent

seldom occurs in stone districts. Usually such a combination is found in places like Gloucestershire, caught between the stone uplands and the timber plain. Stone houses were rare until the seventeenth century except among the gentry. In the early seventeenth century the prosperous farmers-cum-clothiers of the Halifax area who had previously used timber now exploited local stone. Later that century there was also much stone building along the limestone belt from Lincolnshire to Dorset. In most upland and moorland districts such as Dartmoor, the Isle of Man, North Wales and the Scottish Highlands, cottages were built of un-quarried stone. These had dry-stone walls over two feet thick, often plastered or whitewashed and roofed in thatch or stone slates. In Derbyshire and Stafford-shire cottages have large ashlar door jambs and window frames constructed with big stones bonded into rubble walls. Windows are unmoulded and gables are seldom taken above the roof. The care-fully coursed and dressed ashlar, or stones prepared for building, of the Great House was rare in cottages.

Characteristic tile hanging at Biddenden, Kent

*A cottage typical of Oxfordshire with fine
stone walls, simple drip-mouldings above the
windows and doors, and a thatch roof*

In the sixteenth, seventeenth and eighteenth centuries many wealthy men had houses built of unbaked earth. This was known as cob throughout most of southern England and as wichert in Buckinghamshire; it was a mixture of mud, straw and often chalk or small stones and it was primarily the material of the poor, superseded only by the mass-produced bricks of the nineteenth century. Cob cottages built without a timber frame are invariably whitewashed or colour-washed, except for a tarred plinth projecting just above the ground. A thatch roof is brought down low over the eaves and carried in scallops around the upper windows. They are found mainly in Dorset, Devon, Somerset and Wiltshire.

Cottage built of Wiltshire limestone, at Stockton in the Wylye Valley. This type of cottage walled with random rubble and often roofed with thatch is found in the counties traversed or crossed by the limestone belt, such as Dorset, northwest Wiltshire, Somerset, Gloucestershire, Oxfordshire, Leicestershire, Northamptonshire and Lincolnshire.

A sixteenth-century house built in Culross, Fife, Scotland. The stepped projections on the sloping sides of the gables known as the crow-steps, were particularly suited to the granite stone used for building in many parts of Scotland. The stepped parapet was built to stop the wind getting under the tiles of the gable end and ripping them off the roof. There are numerous examples of housing in East Anglia with stepped gables, but in brick, not granite.

Stone-built thatched-roofed home of the late sixteenth century, at Lower Horslake, Devon

Seventeenth-century house at Thrangholm, Dalston, Cumbria. It is built of red sandstone rubble with grey sandstone dressings.

The Romans had used river clay for bricks but it was not until the thirteenth century that river clay was used again, and then mainly in the low-lying areas around London and the eastern counties. In the sixteenth century it was imported and expensive, and became the luxury material of the nouveau riche. Most houses in towns were built entirely of timber but brick or stone was made compulsory for building in the City of London following the Great Fire (1666) and by the eighteenth century they were universally employed.

Until the invention of the Hoffmann Kiln (1858) bricks were made by hand and were uneven with delightful colouring from the firing of the different local clays. The curved brick gables of Norfolk, Essex and Kent are a subtle detail created by the Flemish bricklayers who crossed to Elizabethan England by way of Sandwich in Kent and the East Anglian ports. In East Anglia many cottages were built of flints but windows and doors were squared off with brickwork.

Farmhouse built in Addingham, West Yorkshire in 1670. It is built of rubble laid in courses.

Decorative thatching, Suffolk

House built of coursed rubble at Honeybourne, Hereford and Worcester, in the late seventeenth century

Thatching, Frampton-on-Severn, Gloucestershire

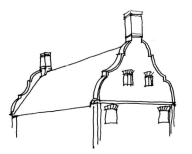

An eighteenth-century Lincolnshire house with Dutch gabling. The influence of trade with the Low Countries is very strong in the Trent Valley. A ship's captain bringing his vessel up to Gainsborough, the limit for sea-going ships, sailed past houses very similar to those he had left at Rotterdam as M. W. Barley points out in his book The English Farmhouse and Cottage.

Most medieval cottages were roofed in thatch, and later with the plain tile. Pantiles, originally imported from Flanders in the twelfth century, were used extensively in those districts that had close commercial ties with Holland. The Lake District produced several varieties of slate and in fourteenth-century Chester Welsh slates were already in use. Yet in late-nineteenth-century Scotland, cottages on the stormy Atlantic coast were still thatched with heather held in place by weighted ropes. But the development of canals and railways, the growth of heavy industry and the use of the mass-produced brick in the housing and factories of the new towns, soon obscured these regional styles.

Characteristic Cottages and Small Houses

The most primitive and perhaps the humblest of all dwellings were the shielings of Northumberland, Cumbria and the Scottish Highlands and Islands. The seasonal migration of pastoral people with their herds from a winter settlement to the summer pastures still predominates in the highland areas of Europe but in the Middle Ages it was a widespread practice over most of northern England. The summer pastures were some distance from the winter settlement so the herdsmen erected a primitive shelter called the shieling. They were generally one- or two-room huts of rectangular shape. The average size was 20 feet by 10 feet. Most were built of drystone walling but some were constructed of turf and had gable walls and a roof of thin timbers and turf. The entrance door was a small gap in the middle of the long wall, few had windows and the fire was in an open hearth along one of the end walls.

While many cruck-framed turf houses were still being used in the Scottish Lowlands in the late eighteenth century, it was a more typical method of building in southern England during the Middle

Shieling in the northern border country. Note the turf roof.

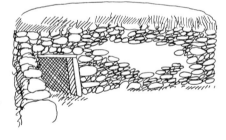

Exposed cruck frame from a demolished house. Wooden forks or crucks are shaped in a slight curve, each pair of timbers forming the split halves of the same tree trunk. They were joined at the apex and supported a horizontal ridge pole which carried the rafters. The space between two pairs of crucks was known as a bay. Usually sixteen feet wide it represented the normal stabling accommodation for two pairs of oxen. Grain or hay was measured by the bay while later medieval houses were assessed for taxation by the number of forks. The one-bay cottage was the humblest and smallest product of cruck framing.

Plans of single-room and two-room shielings

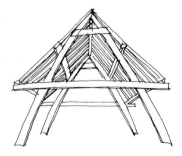

Cruck house in Nottinghamshire

Ages. Then the humblest and smallest house was the single-room cottage built of crucks. While this was undoubtedly the simplest structure to be made from the timber available, the size of each unit, sixteen feet in length, was the normal stabling accommodation for two pairs of oxen, and as a building, was easy to extend. Grain was measured by the bay while some houses were assessed for taxation by the number of crucks.

The poor man's modest means necessitated a simple roof structure of moderate span. The longhouse or laithe house was one room deep with rooms arranged in a row. The family lived at the high end, animals at the lower end. A variation on this theme is to be found in Yorkshire. The dwelling called a coit, was combined under one roof with a barn.

In the crofting communities of the Scottish islands the black houses are found. These are built to cope with the Atlantic winds and have no corners or gables. They have a double skin of dry-stone walling filled with earth, rubble or

House-and-byre homestead, Powys, Wales. A structural break between house and byre is usual. Unlike the traditional longhouse of Dartmoor, there is often no common ridgeline to the roof.

33

Right. *The classic longhouse which began to appear in the uplands of Devonshire in the late fifteenth and early sixteenth century. The house was usually two storeys, or one storey with an attic. The central open hearth was later replaced by a chimney. A cross passage and the chimney separated the house from the byre.*

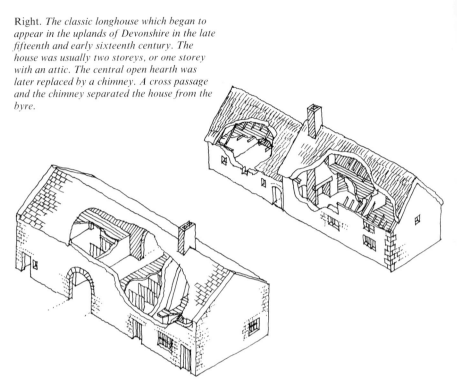

Above. *Laithe house of West Yorkshire in the late eighteenth century. Early longhouses were the houses of men at a very low economic level, with provision for a few animals. The laithe house was a product of the hilly country bordering the industrial areas of West Yorkshire. The considerable affluence of the smallholders here by 1700 was based on the* increasing market for their dairy products as well as a supplementary income from the 'putting out' system of the woollen industry. The laithe house was a combination of barn and byre, and the barn was as important as the byre unlike the longhouse. A prominent feature was a high arched entrance into the laithe to allow a loaded hay-sled to pass beneath.

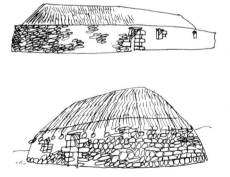

Black house, Lewis

Black house, Skye. Note the difference between the two houses. The Hebridean type of house at Lewis provides no eaves to the roof. Instead the roof springs from the inner sections of the wall leaving a broad surface of wall top exposed. In the Skye type the hipped-ended roof has overhanging eaves.

peat. There are no windows or chimneys and the central fireplace is vented through a hole in the roof. Byre and living room are under the same roof. In the early days there was no partition to screen the cow from a view of the fire.

A characteristic building of parts of Cumbria and Northumberland in the eighteenth and nineteenth centuries was the bastle house. These were built originally in the sixteenth and seventeenth centuries as defensible farmhouses along the troubled border areas with Scotland; they are rectangular in plan, usually 35 feet by 25 feet and built of large irregular

Bastle, Gatehouse, Tarset, Northumberland.

Bastle, Akeld, Northumberland. It has four-feet-thick walls of random rubble with free-stone dressings and some large boulders on the base course. The external stair is a late addition. The lower storey is covered by a barrel vault pierced by a ladder hole.

blocks of stone. They are two storeys in height with steeply-pitched gables. The ground floor was used for animals while the upper floor, entered through an external stone staircase, was the living quarters. Windows were few and small. Fireplaces were built at the gable ends usually with a timber-framed and wattle-and-daubed hood. Roofs were originally thatched but later many were slated.

The enclosures and subsequent merging of the farms meant that many village-street farms became redundant. They were converted into the maximum number of cottages together with their barns and cowhouses. The converted cottages were then rented. But the seventeenth-century farmer realized that he could not keep his labour force without building cottages for them and soon the tied cottage was developed for the married labourer. The single man lived in his employer's house; from the Elizabethan period onwards the yeomen's houses had chambers or parlours for servants. Nearly every farmhouse in the East Midlands used garrets for bedrooms.

Rows or terraces of cottages belong to the late eighteenth century. Many were only one-and-a-half storeys high, with dormer windows in the thatched roof. They were usually one room wide but

Plan of typical bastle house

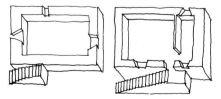

Early eighteenth-century labourers' terrace housing

Gothic Revival Lodge, late eighteenth century

there was often a second, smaller service room, sometimes added in an outshut later.

The major distinction at the turn of the nineteenth century was between the open village, where land could be bought or rented for building, and those which were closed and belonged to one owner who would control its development. The model cottages of Milton Abbas in Dorset were laid out in 1775 to rehouse families evicted when the original village was demolished because it interrupted the view from the landlord's houses.

The cult of the picturesque produced its own distinctive forms, like the Gothic Revival lodge, culled from the latest of the pattern books, and in vogue in the late eighteenth and early nineteenth centuries. This was the period of the expansion of the weaving industry throughout southeast Lancashire. The old loom shops could not cope with the work so new weavers' cottages with loom shops were built. Characteristic features of these cottages are the spinning galleries and the large windows.

A particular product of the rapidly-expanding urban centres of the industrial north were the rows of terrace housing of the early nineteenth century. One typical development was the back-to-back house which produced the unhealthy slums of the late nineteenth century.

The dairy at Blaise Castle, Avon. Designed by John Nash in 1802, it was the first building on the estate to introduce the cottage ornée style. Blaise Hamlet itself consists of nine cottages in a picturesque style built around a green.

Back-to-back housing

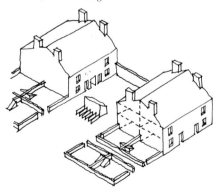

Plans

Richard Carew in his *Survey of Cornwall* (*c.* 1580) described the Cornish husbandmen's houses in the early sixteenth century as having walls of earth and ground-floor rooms with few partitions, open to the low thatched roofs. There were no glass windows and scarcely a chimney other than a hole in the wall to let out the smoke. There were similar houses in Cumbria in the late seventeenth century and early eighteenth century.

Stone-walled cottages were as limited in plan as any built with wattle and daub because the small rural builder did not have the ability to build a roof spanning more than one room. Any enlargement was made either by adding another bay or by building outwards within an outshut under a lean-to roof.

In planning, the important decisions

A mid-sixteenth-century farmhouse in Wickham, Hampshire. The most usual way of extending a house was by building an additional bay at the end, as in the cruck house and traditional longhouse, or by means of an extension at the rear in an outshut which can be seen in this example.

concerned the positioning of the fire-place, the entrance and, where the house had an upper floor, the position of the staircase. Many houses were built on sloping ground. The upper end was used for domestic purposes and the lower end for the dirtier chores of the house or farm. The major plan form was based on the concept of the house as a hall, with the ground-floor room open to the roof. A floor was added at one end at a later date. A fireplace was the next development, separating the hall from the storeyed end by a passage. The second-storeyed end of the typical Kentish yeoman's house was later added to this plan. Such developments began with the patrician's house, passing eventually to the smaller house and cottage.

The humblest plan was the single unit.

Plan of a laithe house, Dinckley, Lancashire

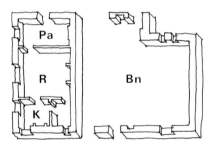

Cruck-built open hall house. Typical of the fifteenth century, they are less spacious than two-storey houses of timber-frame construction. The fire was in an open hearth in the centre of the hall. The open hall, common to all medieval dwellings of any size, was the largest and most important room in the house where the whole household gathered.

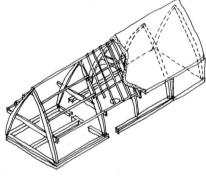

Laithe house, Todmorden, West Yorkshire. The laithe house combines a dwelling and barn and byre under one roof. The combination of barn and byre is the laithe. Separate doorways lead to the house and the laithe. Sometimes the two may be connected. Late-eighteenth-century and early-nineteenth-century laithe houses were built by smallholders farming recently-enclosed or divided lands on the fringes of the moors.

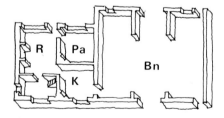

House plans showing one single cell divided by partitions into a larger and a smaller room. Where later additions were added at the end a cross passage was invariably incorporated.

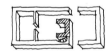

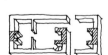

This later developed into the two-unit house, comprising a large room and small room divided by a partition. Above was a loft. The fireplace was on the end wall by the entrance. Later extensions, usually service rooms, would be added with a through passage in line with the structure. The passage separated the service rooms from the main area behind the fireplace. As bedrooms were built within the roof, a

House with a through passage behind the chimney stack and fireplace

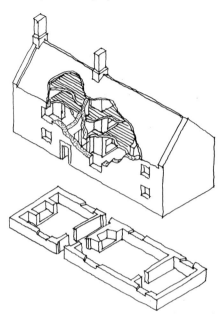

In these plans a cross passage was included within the original unit. Along the open side of the passage was the main living room. Behind the partitions on the other side was a storage room. Later this was heated. Bedrooms were in the roof space.

The plan forms here revolved round the position of the central fireplace. Living room and service rooms were heated by two fire-places built back-to-back. Entry to the house was through a lobby beside the fire. The staircase to the upper rooms was positioned to one side of the fire or built in an outshut at the back of the house.

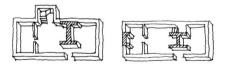

By the early seventeenth century larger houses were planned two-rooms deep. The ground-floor plan usually consisted of a main living room, another private room, a kitchen and a service room. A staircase at the back led to the upper floors. In other examples the staircase would be planned between the two main rooms.

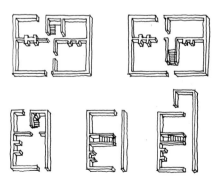

House of one-and-a-half storeys. Dormer windows were usually installed to give more light to loft spaces when eventually converted to bedrooms.

staircase would be squeezed in beside the fireplace or built in a projection out from the main plan. A variation was the plan with a passage running across the structure. Rooms were heated by a central fireplace. Cottages based on these plans are usually found in the lowland counties of England.

Both plan types were adapted for the development of the square-planned, double-fronted house. This was two rooms deep with a rear staircase which was later centralized. The single-fronted terrace cottages of the industrial towns were a development of this plan. Another variation was the single-fronted back-to-back house which had no through ventilation. It was possible to build extensions on to all but the back-to-back house.

The first-floor plan is much rarer. The upper floor hall house of the aristocrat of Norman times, or the fourteenth- and fifteenth-century tower house, the peel tower, built for defensive purposes along the troubled border areas with Wales and Scotland, are examples.

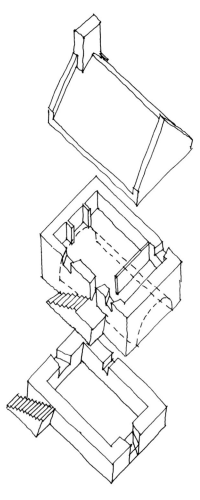

Plan of a first-floor house – bastle house, Northumberland. Originally entry to the first floor would have been by a ladder from the ground floor. The external staircase was a later addition.

Walling

There were two methods used by the designer – mass construction and frame construction. Where earth, brick and stone were available mass construction was possible while timber was needed for frame construction. The cottager in the Middle Ages used earth and timber as these materials were the most he could afford. It was rare for the cottage before the eighteenth and nineteenth centuries to have been built of very substantial materials. Most medieval cottages were flimsy affairs built at night on the village common. In timber regions more substantial cottages were constructed either with a cruck or a box frame.

Elizabethan cottages were of box-frame construction made of large timbers, closely spaced. Increasing demand for timber by the shipbuilders and iron-smelting industries forced builders to use lighter timbers, with squarer panels. The panels between the timber frames were usually filled with wattle and daub, which consists of a foundation of timber stakes woven with branches and reeds to form a basketweave which is covered with a mixture of clay, dung and horsehair. The panels were liable to deteriorate and over the years in the late seventeenth century many were replaced by bricks sometimes laid in patterns; this is called brick nogging. Other materials, such as slate or thin stone slabs, have been used, but in narrower panels.

When clay roofing tiles became cheap and easily available, they were used in preference as they provided a better weather protection to timber-frame walls. Various shaped tiles, developed mostly in the counties of Kent and East and West Sussex in the early nineteenth century, were moulded creating intricate and interesting patterns on walls. Where an existing timber-frame building with a jettied upper floor was clad, a brick wall

Cruck-frame house. The infill panels were usually wattle and daub.

Sweet Briar Hall, built at Nantwich, Cheshire in the late sixteenth century. The front is panel framed, the rear is in small framing.

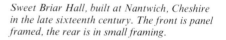

a. *Large framing was, before 1450, the commonest form of framing, usually left as open as possible, strengthened or decorated with braces.* b. *Small framing was rare before the middle of the fifteenth century. The framing is small, usually two panels per storey. It is a characteristic of the western part of England.* c. *Close studding was formed when the frame was divided into narrow panels by studs. It originated in the southeast and was essentially a decorative form of framing. It was the most expensive method of framing in the late Middle Ages and was used in the building of houses for the wealthy and more status conscious.* d. *The basic framework was further subdivided to form more intricate and decorative patterns. By the seventeenth and eighteenth centuries when the houses of the well-to-do were being built in brick and stone, instead of timber, poorer and less substantial framing techniques were employed to build the houses of the poor. Imported softwoods were by now common in the south and east. The frames were rarely exposed, the norm being a covering of plaster, tiles or weatherboarding.*

Wattle and daub. This eventually deteriorated and was invariably replaced by panels of brick, called brick nogging.

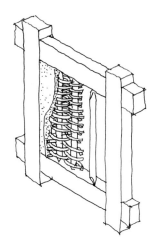

a.

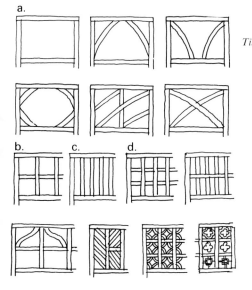

b.   **c.**   **d.**

Tile hanging

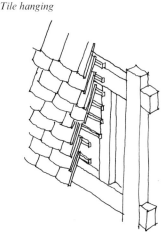

Left. *Mid-seventeenth-century timber-framed house, Old Harlow, Essex*

was often built in front of the ground-floor timbers. Brick had become the universal building material despite the Brick Taxes (1784–1850). The mathematical tile, introduced in the southeastern counties during the late eighteenth century, was a cheap means of producing a fashionable brick appearance while avoiding the taxes. The façades of many timber-frame buildings of Kent and Sussex towns were refaced with mathematical tiling. Towards the end of the eighteenth century oak or elm weatherboarding was used as an alternative

Burgh Hall, Swaffham Bulbeck, Cambridgeshire. From the early sixteenth century, narrow close studding in East Anglia is found more often on large houses such as Burgh Hall, on communal or special-purpose buildings such as the old Wool Hall, Lavenham, Suffolk, or on town houses like the Paycocke's House Coggeshall, Essex.

Mathematical tiling

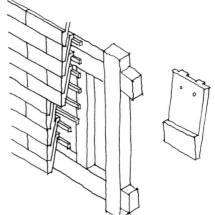

A seventeenth-century example of close studding in North Yorkshire

cladding material. This is mainly seen in southeast England, and it was primarily confined to small houses and cottages. Many timber-frame houses were covered with an unbroken cladding of lime plaster on a wooden lath and there would be a separate lath-and-plaster interior. Dur-ing the sixteenth, seventeenth and early eighteenth centuries decorative patterns were achieved by incised or raised plaster relief work. This is called pargeting.

Cobbles and pebbles were used for walling and the walls are usually rendered and whitewashed. Pebbles were nearly

Brick nogging at Weedon, Buckinghamshire

Plaster cladding on wooden lathing. The framing would be covered over.

a. *Random rubble walling*
b. *Rubble walling laid in courses*

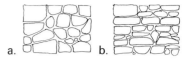

a.   b.

Different types of walling:
a. *Galleting in rubble masonry*
b. *Horizontal lacing courses of brick through flint walling*
c. *Tracery of thin limestone combined with flint*

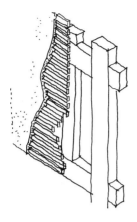

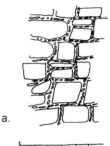

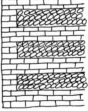

a.

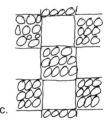

b.

c.

always laid in courses. Window and door openings were invariably squared off with brickwork. This is a characteristic of cottages in East Anglia and the southeast.

Dry-stone walling was used mainly for enclosing fields although some of the black houses of the Hebrides are built of dry-stone walls. The most primitive of walling materials was unbaked earth (cob or wichert) or turf. The cob cottages of Devon were built without a frame. The walls were shuttered when the mixture was placed in a wooden formwork while it was drying, and built in depths of two feet at a time. Turf walls, found in nineteenth-century Ireland and parts of Scotland, were usually made of blocks six inches deep and about three feet by two feet in size, the roof frequently being carried on crucks.

The Roof

Today one of the simplest ways of providing a roof is to span from wall to wall with timber joists, and then to cover the boards with bituminous felt, asphalt or metal. The flat roof freed the plan but for the medieval carpenter things were not so easy.

Timber was plentiful, but the lengths available limited the spans the carpenters could build without more complex framing. The type of construction was also affected by the choice of roof covering. All materials had an appropriate pitch. A tiled roof, for example, had to have a steeper pitch than a slate roof, but slates, such as the Welsh slate, were heavier than the clay tiles and so larger roof timbers were necessary. Slate and pantiles were more appropriate for gables while thatch and tiles were more appropriate for hipped roofs. Where there was a choice then fashion was the main influence. In East Anglia the result was Dutch gabling and pantiled roofs. Classical lines were more fashionable for the houses of the prosperous Georgians during the Industrial Revolution and a low-pitched slate roof was chosen because it could more easily be hidden behind a raised parapet which gave clean lines to the house fronts.

Before the development of the mansard roof in the late sixteenth century the carpenter would, in some instances, have been preoccupied in providing sufficient headroom in the loft space for sleeping. The mansard roof is a roof which is sometimes gabled and has a relatively flat-topped upper slope with a steeper lower slope and this usually contains

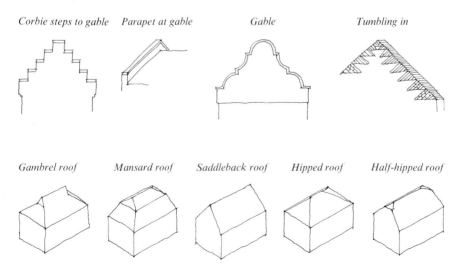

Corbie steps to gable   *Parapet at gable*   *Gable*   *Tumbling in*

Gambrel roof   *Mansard roof*   *Saddleback roof*   *Hipped roof*   *Half-hipped roof*

Cruck-frame house at Didbrook, Gloucestershire

dormers for the use of the attic space.

The early frame buildings were of cruck construction. Like the twentieth-century 'A' frame house, the crucks provided an integral framing for both wall and roof. All that was needed was a cover. The usual roofing material during the Middle Ages was thatch but by the seventeenth and eighteenth centuries thatch was only used for the humblest dwellings.

The early turf- or stone-built houses usually had a single roof consisting only of the sloping timbers known as rafters. This restricted the plan as great spans were not possible. Where a plan had to be extended it always followed the direction of the structure, making the plan long and narrow. Where greater spans were required, making the rafters by themselves inadequate, a beam or purlin was placed under them to give support. This is called

Detail of roof trusses:

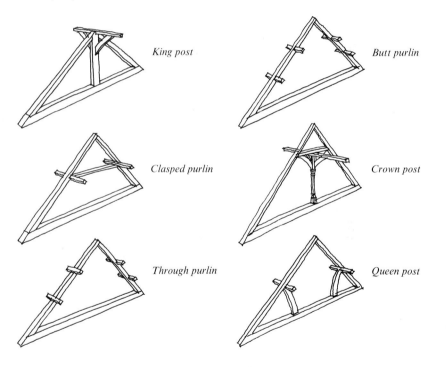

King post

Butt purlin

Clasped purlin

Crown post

Through purlin

Queen post

During the thirteenth century the English carpenters began to use long lengths of timber to stabilize the rafters. This was either done by providing a ridge piece fixed to the rafters at their apex, by tying the rafters along their sides by means of purlins, or by providing a collar purlin running along it below the collars which tied the rafters. The collar purlin was

usually supported by a vertical timber called a crown post rising from the tie beam. The ridge in cruck building is carried by the cruck blades but a king post supported the ridge of many northern roofs. Where side purlins were necessary they were carried either by principal rafters, by cruck blades, by queen posts or clasped between principal rafter and collar.

a double roof. The purlins spanned from wall to wall but where this was not possible then support for the purlins was given by trusses carried on walls or columns. There are two variations: one is the butt purlin roof. Here the purlin runs between the principal rafters with the common rafters passing above. The purlins are supported by a roof truss. It is usually associated with box-frame construction, the tie beam of the box frame acting as a tie beam for the roof truss. The second, associated with cruck construction, is the through purlin. Here there are no principal rafters, only common rafters. The purlin, which supports the rafters, is itself carried on the back of the truss.

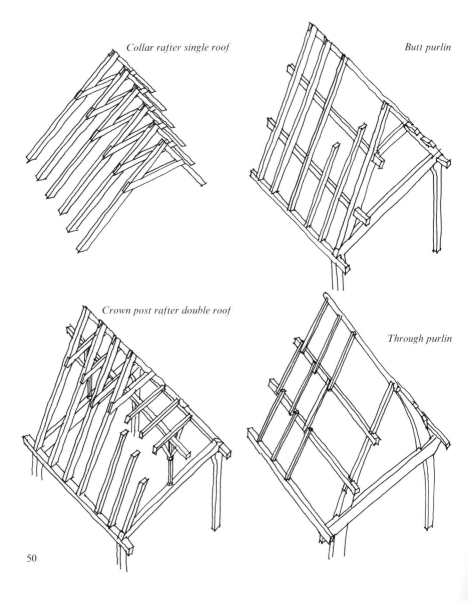

Collar rafter single roof

Butt purlin

Crown post rafter double roof

Through purlin

Details

Life for many cottagers was hard and, before the arrival of the pattern books, there was little time, interest or money for the current trends in architectural styles. Details were of the barest necessary, much being left to the nature of the materials themselves. In thatching, hazel spars were used to give a variety of patterns at ridge, verge and eaves. Every thatcher had his own individual style, easily adapted to current architectural fashions. In Devon there are low-pitched thatch roofs with rounded ends. In East Anglia the pitch is higher and the ends are often gabled.

In the eastern and southeastern counties early plain tiles were handmade; later multi-coloured or specially-shaped tiles were used to create varying patterns and textures for the roof. The same applied to the walling of the timber-frame house. Another decorative walling finish is pargeting which is an ornamental design in plaster relief. It was fashionable in East

Typical Norfolk gable end showing pronounced Flemish interest. The diagonal coursing to the brickwork at the gable parapet is known as 'tumbled in'.

Details of stepped gable on a cottage at Bawburgh, Norfolk

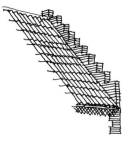

Use of a simple geometrical design for pargeting ornament on a late-seventeenth-century cottage at Nayland, Suffolk.

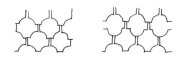

Various patterns of tile hanging

Anglia between the sixteenth and eighteenth centuries and its origins are found in the incised work which takes the form of combed decoration.

Although the Great Houses already had chimneys by the mid-fifteenth century, the smaller houses and cottages seldom had chimneys before the reign of Elizabeth I. The cottage fire was still laid in the centre of the room on the bare earth floor, the smoke escaping as best it could. Later a hole was made in the roof. But the ever-present danger of fire in the Middle Ages made the brick chimney necessary. Brick resisted heat better than stone, and

it gave better opportunities for displays of craftsmanship. In the timber areas of the Midlands, East Anglia and the south, chimneys were, for structural reasons, built in the centre of the house. In the seventeenth century, Kent and Sussex chimneys were often set anglewise to their base; in East Anglia planning was predominantly symmetrical. In the stone regions of the Lake District massive chimney-breasts are found built externally. Undressed stone was usually used and a circular stack was the only way to avoid jointing problems at the corners. Where down draughts were a problem a

Pricked and scratched patterns gave decorative textures to plastered walls. Another method, as in this cottage at Chiddingstone, Kent, was to panel the rough plaster surfaces by forming narrow smooth divisions by pressing flat boards between. The use of diapering, as in the example here, is rare.

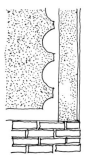

Decorative Tudor chimney stacks of the great houses

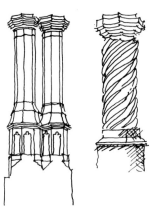

Various patterns used in decorative plaster combing, East Anglia

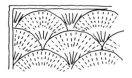

simple device of tilting two stone slabs against one another over the top of the shaft or by raising a single slab supported on the four corners was used. By the nineteenth century chimney pots were being manufactured.

Many of the Great Houses had ornamental leadwork guttering by the seventeenth century but it was not until the late nineteenth century that gutters were added to cottages. This normally happened when the thatching was taken off and the roof tiled.

Cottage windows were few and small. The extra cost of casements meant that most were fixed, the entrance door and chimney flue providing the necessary ventilation. Casement windows in stone-built cottages had moulded stone mullions separating the lights or divisions of the window. The Dutch sash window, which is a sliding wooden-framed window, was introduced in the seventeenth century while some mid-nineteenth-century estate cottages, fashioned on the pattern books, adopted the oriel window which projected from the upper floor. In the Lake District a rare feature was the spinning gallery where, weather permitting, the spinning wheel was operated.

A seventeenth-century chimney stack, Suffolk. Note the positioning of the flue which is diagonal on plan.

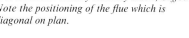

Windows on a house at Trawden, Lancashire in the early seventeenth century

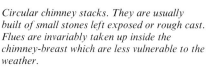

Detail of a window in a house built in 1631 at Brighouse, West Yorkshire

Circular chimney stacks. They are usually built of small stones left exposed or rough cast. Flues are invariably taken up inside the chimney-breast which are less vulnerable to the weather.

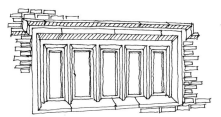

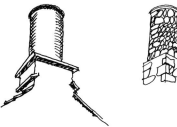

A late-eighteenth-century sash window with Gothic Revival top

Oriel window, Theale, Reading, Berkshire

Early-nineteenth-century sliding sash window

Oriel window, West Wycombe, Buckinghamshire

Late-nineteenth-century sash window

Spinning gallery, Cumbria

Early-nineteenth-century Gothic Revival window

Right. *A timber-framed cottage with decoratively-carved barge boards at Weobley, in Hereford and Worcester*

Detail of a stone doorway of a house at Trawden, Lancashire, built in the early seventeenth century

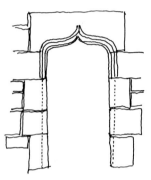

In the humbler house during the Middle Ages, doors were usually fixed direct to the wall. Later the door was set in a frame. Where mouldings were possible they resembled those of the windows. In the stone regions of the Pennines, the decorated lintel is a characteristic detail, the lintel being the slab of

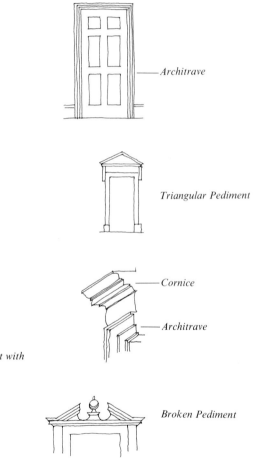

Architrave

Triangular Pediment

Cornice

Architrave

Detail of a stone doorway of a late-seventeenth-century house at Yaxley, Cambridgeshire

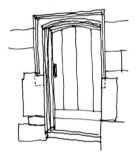

Broken Pediment

Stepped Voussoirs

Cottage door, Marston Magna, Somerset with drip moulding

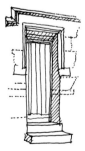

stone across an opening supported on columns or by the wall. During the late eighteenth and early nineteenth centuries architraves, pediments and stepped voussoirs or stones used in arches faithfully imitating classical examples were used in the grander cottage. Elaborate porches were built. Decorative work was often carved by the craftsmen. The picturesque cottage had elaborately carved barge boards; these are the wooden boards which cover the gable beams outside. Often corner posts were carved with figure sculptures and floral designs. The non-loadbearing partition walls were usually decoratively panelled.

Mid-eighteenth-century doorway showing influence of the Renaissance

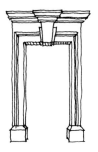

A nineteenth-century porch and door, Wiltshire

Late-eighteenth-century door, Wales

Quoins: the prepared stonework or brickwork at corners of buildings:

Brick quoin with flint

Stone quoin with brick

A nineteenth-century door, Cumbria

Ashlar quoin with rubble

When the open hall was ceiled over the beams carrying the intermediate floor were sometimes moulded.

A feature of most cottages was the compactness of plan. Few had store cupboards, larders or sculleries. The bake oven, positioned by the fire, was usually built within the wall itself or projecting out from the main house.

Arch

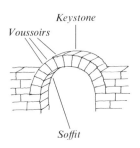

Distinctive details were in the ways stairs were added to houses. Characteristic of parts of the Lake District is the external staircase. This example is in Hawkshead, Lancashire.

Outside stair to a fisherman's house, St Ives, Cornwall

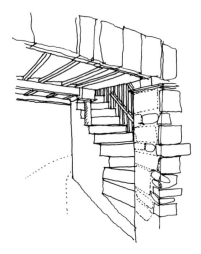

The Interior

Until the beginning of the fifteenth century peasants lived in one-room huts, built of mud and thatched with reeds or straw. Eventually these were replaced by the two-room cottage which consisted of the hall, containing the hearth, and the bower or chamber which provided sleeping accommodation. The rooms were open to the rafters, while the floor was earth. The fire was laid in the centre of the room either on the bare earth or in a flat iron pan. Before chimneys were built the smoke, in finding the best way out, blackened most of the roof timbers and much of the walls. Windows, unglazed, at this time were used more for ventilation than for lighting. Cloth or canvas blinds were used to close them. Rushes were sometimes strewn on the floor to keep it clean and to provide more comfort. One of the inconveniences of the earth floor was that, periodically, it had to be dug up. The porous floor absorbed filth in the form of nitrous matters and it was from such a source that the nitre, necessary for the manufacture of gunpowder, was collected. A good floor finish was obtained by mixing bullocks' blood with mud. In later cottages, flagstones, bricks and quarry tiles were used.

The fifteenth-century cottage was scantily furnished, usually with home-made funiture consisting of a coffer or cupboard, a trestle table, some stools or a bench. Utensils such as wooden platters and earthenware pitchers, and cooking implements were homemade by the cottager or by the village blacksmith. Later in the sixteenth century when sycamore was introduced to Britain this clean, white wood was used for making kitchen implements such as wooden spoons and rolling pins. When the weather was fine meals were probably prepared outside.

During the long winter evenings the cottager was busy with the crafts necessary to keep him above subsistence level. The women spun and wove wool into cloth and hemp into linen on the spinning wheels and the men fashioned the farm implements and made the kitchen utensils.

The cottage was extended by adding another bay or by building a service room in an outshut under a lean-to roof. The open hall was gradually chambered over and a ladder or staircase provided.

A funnel was provided in the sixteenth century to carry off the smoke. It was built of wood, mud or lath and plaster. In medieval cottages a large hood sometimes projected in front of the fireplace to catch the smoke. This was replaced when the whole chimney-breast was brought forward. Many fireplace openings are six feet or more in width and the hearth is usually raised. An adjustable swinging-arm pot crane allowed for several hanging pots. The convenience of the cooking fireplace later replaced open-fire cooking. To one side of the fireplace would be the bake-oven which was usually hollowed out in the thickness of the wall or built projecting on the outside.

Furniture such as cupboards, beds and benches were built in to save space. The parlour found in the larger house was not found until the model cottages were built in the nineteenth century. Few of the bedrooms had fireplaces at this time.

By the turn of the twentieth century some were still living in primitive turf or mud-walled cottages without running water or sanitation as in Ireland or the Isle of Man. Other people have so extended, altered and modernized their cottages that they appear more like villas than the utilitarian dwellings most had once been. While modern comforts are a must, many baulk at a modern interior and sport, instead, the horse brasses, William Morris wallpapers and the rest of the picturesque ensemble. It does not

The Summer Kitchen. When the weather was fine the meals were prepared outside.

The interior of an ironstone miner's cottage in Coalbrookdale, Salop

matter that these are equally different to the traditional cottage interior. Somehow they smack of craftsmanship and the so-called 'good old days', and that is sufficient. No one seems to want to adopt the *real* cottage interior. For some all this is reactionary twaddle. These critics adopt more modish interiors, in many instances because it is more economic. They build themselves whole new cottages. The *new* cottage is an open-plan house, starkly modern in every respect with glass walls and a flat roof. Inside there are few walls, most areas are simply screened off by furniture or light partitions. Despite the modern design, however, this new house is really far from new. It is certainly no fake; that is something good that can be said for it.

But what is remarkable is its similarity to the traditional single-cell house, still to be found in parts of Wales today, where the dresser or cupboard is used to divide one area from another. The sophisticated built-in furniture of the modern house is little different in principle to the box beds and built-in cupboards found in many of the black houses in Skye. What has really changed is the technology, the materials and society. Everything is perfectly acceptable, but one thing: the new modern cottage of today with all its sophistication and wall-to-wall comfort is often alien in the rural scene. And this regard or disregard for context is a major problem of building design in the twentieth century.

Cottage Gardens

The cottage garden originated out of necessity. The Black Death, or bubonic plague, in the mid-fourteenth century killed off about a third of the population and sometimes whole communities and villages. This led to a scarcity of labour and landlords were therefore forced to let their lands to tenants as an inducement to work. The plot of land let to the tenants later developed into the cottage garden; it was generally a rectangular piece of about four acres and a large part was given over to beans for flour and later, rye, barley or oats. In the first instance the landlords would have provided the seeds but usually most plants such as strawberries, gooseberries and currants would be collected from the wild. Apart from an apple tree fairly near the cottage, the rest of the land would be devoted to growing staple vegetables such as cabbages, broad beans, turnips, onions and leeks. Herbs such as violets, borage, bergamot, chervil and majoram were grown and provided the only flowers found in cottage gardens at this time. Even the lovely traditional cottage flower, the Madonna Lily, was grown only for the ointment that could be made from its bulb. The monastery or physic garden where the monks grew plants for medicinal purposes probably gave rise to the traditional cottage garden.

Cottagers' gardens provided their main source of food; every inch was valuable and not to be wasted on new-fangled crops which might fail. There was therefore little change in the crops grown in gardens from the fourteenth to nineteenth centuries. Meat was expensive and poaching a risky business, so cottagers had little need of the herbs and spices, and exotic fruits to be found growing at the manor house. They were also very wary of new tastes; it took, for example, nearly two centuries for potatoes to become popular in England. The Irish, however, grew potatoes in the 1500s but it was not until the 1680s that the more affluent Lancashire workers grew them. By the mid-eighteenth century potatoes were found in the north of England and Wales, and by the end of the century in East Anglia.

However, there was a drastic change between 1760 and 1867, due to the Acts of Enclosure. Parliament enclosed seven million acres of common land on the grounds that this would produce more efficient farming. The cottager was deprived of his grazing rights and his four acres of land around the cottage became reduced to about half an acre. The Acts provided allotment gardens in compensation but this was poor justice if one considers that between 1845 and 1867 half a million acres were enclosed and only 2,000 acres given over as allotments.

Cottagers from time to time had their ornamental flings, one of them being topiary. This form of decorative hedge cutting became, during the reign of William and Mary (1689–1702), highly fashionable in the great gardens and since most cottages already had protective hedging established, it seemed natural to have a go at topiary, especially since it cost nothing but the labour. Cottagers continued this craft long after the sweeping changes of William Kent and Capability Brown in the grand gardens during the eighteenth century, and it is still to be seen occasionally today.

Flowers eventually crept into cottage gardens, pushed into awkward corners and odd pockets of soil, probably by the

A nineteenth-century cottage and its garden where kale can be seen growing.

cottager's wife. There was usually a straight path to the door and sweet-scented herbs like thyme, rosemary, lavenders and mints would border it intermingling with the salad crops and cabbages. Pinks, wallflowers, sweet williams, hollyhocks, tulips, blue lupins, pansies and roses all found enough space among the vegetables to thrive. It is due to the cottage gardener that many of our native plants and flowers have survived. Primulas for example and freak primroses dug up from the wild, survived and slowly developed into the richly-coloured polyanthus we know today. As the rich man discarded the old plants in favour of new varieties, the poor man filled his garden with them by way of gifts from the head gardener of the grand house and so the cottager unwittingly turned his plot into a small plant museum.

Today, the very words 'cottage garden' conjure up visions of colourful, scented flowers spilling over paths and out of tubs, white-painted picket fences, rustic seats, rockeries, and honeysuckle and

Topiary in a cottage garden at Basing in Hampshire

clematis scrambling over the walls. This 'roses-round-the-door' image has been created mainly by the new breed of cottagers – the middle classes. What we know today as a cottage garden is in fact a stylized and somewhat artificial version of the real thing. This can be traced back to the influence of Gertrude Jekyll (1843–1935), a skilful craftswoman and embroidress, whose overwhelming interest in plants and trees led her to devote her life to gardens and their design. She disliked the formality and vulgarity of rich men's gardens, preferring the variety and naturalness of cottage gardens. Her meeting with William Robinson, born in 1839 the son of a poor Irish cottager, was a fusion of two like minds. After starting as a garden boy in Ireland Robinson rose to take charge of the Royal Botanic Society's herbaceous collection, which included native English plants. This led to his collecting plants of the countryside and his increasing admiration for the wild garden. He started a magazine *The Garden*, for which Gertrude Jekyll wrote, and their combined influence on a wide public has become obvious. Some of the famous gardens such as Hidcote, Sissinghurst and Great Dixter, were later fashioned along similar lines.

The cottage garden has survived and almost come a full circle. The herbaceous borders and specimen shrubs are making way for the vegetables, raspberry canes and fruit trees. Radishes, onions, lettuces and parsley once again rub shoulders with the Michaelmas daisies. The cottager is once more turning to his garden as an economic salvation in hard times.

Left. *The cottage path, bordered by vegetables and flowers, is as characteristic a part of the cottage as the building itself.*

Agriculture

During the Dark Ages, the peasant farmer began to colonize the land, wresting it from marsh, wood and sea, or ploughing higher and higher up the moorland slopes. This feverish conversion of the land was only temporarily stopped with the coming of the Black Death (1348–9).

A typical thirteenth- and fourteenth-century moorland house was the longhouse, which consisted of a common entrance for men and cattle, with the domestic quarters at one end, and shippon or byre at the other.

Land fell into fewer hands after the dissolution of the monasteries in the 1530s, which resulted in the subsequent development of the large Tudor estates and the Great Rebuilding. This was followed by the turmoil of the Civil War and then the age of parliamentary enclosure and Georgian prosperity. The big landowners knew how to make a profit out of the land and the small farmer was soon squeezed out. Evicted from the acre or so of arable land farmed by family labour he became a landless labourer dependent on employment on one of the large farms or on the charity of the Poor Relief. Many landless labourers lived in converted stables, storage sheds and outbuildings, or, if single, in the garrets or parlours of the farmhouse. The labourer's cottage was usually a one-and-a-half storey house with two rooms on each floor and often squeezed between farmhouse and barn (*see p. 155*).

It is in the eighteenth century that purpose-built labourers' cottages were first introduced. Long rows of houses were built similar to the purpose-built housing of the nineteenth-century industrial worker. Rows of semi-detached cottages were also erected. But much of this building was in southern England for the northern farmer was concerned more with providing lodging above a barn or byre for unmarried labourers than with building cottages. The cottages that were built were usually smaller than those in the south. Houses were one storey in height, often with only one room. On some of the large nineteenth-century Northumberland farms these one-storeyed, one-roomed houses were built in rows.

Radical developments in housing for the labourer were left to the more enlightened landlords. The eighteenth century was the golden age of landscape design when landlords fashioned their estates along Virgilian lines. The agricultural economy in East Anglia at this time was particularly prosperous, and one landlord, Lord Orford, discovered that his new park and lake at Chippenham, in Cambridgeshire, had swallowed up half the village, so he built a new one in 1712

on lines more suited to his own taste. Norfolk was particularly renowned for the quality of its farm cottages; crusading agricultural reformers, like Coke of Holkham, rich from their profitable new farming methods, could afford to build good-quality cottages.

Following the enclosures many cottages had been demolished and towards the end of the eighteenth century cottagers were increasingly housed in 'model' villages. The best known is that of Nuneham Courtenay (1760) in Oxfordshire. Style was of great importance at this time and the architect took over from the master builder.

Range of cottages built in 1800 at Great Barford, Bedfordshire

House with a bedroom over the byre, northwest Donegal, Ireland

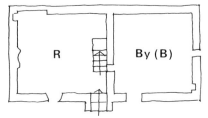

Aisled barn with sleeping quarters at one end, built in 1689 at Dalton, Lancashire

Aisled barn and byre with a house at one end. Built in the eighteenth century at Old Laund Booth, Lancashire.

Cottages at Nuneham Courtenay, Oxfordshire (c. 1760). Each cottage housed two families and all outbuildings were tucked out of sight behind.

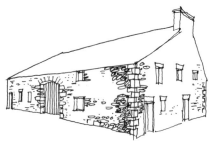

Communications

River traffic was important in Roman and medieval England and by the beginning of the seventeenth century there were about seven hundred miles of navigable rivers, mostly in southern England. Sea coal was the chief cargo, with timber, stone and grain being carried on return. It was not until the building of the canals that a comprehensive transportation system linked the industrial north to the Irish Sea, with Manchester to the east and Liverpool to the west. The Weaver Navigation Scheme was undertaken following the first Canal Act of 1755. It provided an outlet to the Mersey for salt mined in central Cheshire. This was followed by the Sankey (1755–60) and the Bridgewater (1759–65) canals, constructed to serve the Lancashire coalfields. By the 1820s there were over 3,000 miles of canals operating. The canals brought their own special kind of buildings – wharfs, corn mills, inns and, of course, the lock-keepers' cottages. At Stourport, in Hereford and Worcester, a whole town was built in the mid-eighteenth century around the basin that linked the Severn and Stour with James Brindley's canal. Canal building was functional and uniform. Cast iron was used for the window frames, while the openings in cottages and toll houses were standardized. The canal companies invariably used the same details and materials for all buildings.

The Railway Age began in the 1830s with the opening of the first great railway between Manchester and Liverpool. The railways also had their own distinctive buildings – the stations, workshops and

Octagonal tollkeeper's cottage, Yorkshire, 1805

Toll House at Bratch on the Staffordshire and Worcestershire canal

Bridgekeeper's house, Gloucester and Sharpness canal

The Railway Age began in the 1830s with the opening of the first great railway between Manchester and Liverpool.

the railway village. When the Engine Establishment was constructed at Swindon in Wiltshire the company built cottages for its personnel. These were designed by Sir Matthew Digby Wyatt, the architect of Paddington Station. They were built of local stone and varied in size; the corner houses at the end of each street were for the foreman, and therefore larger. But the railways were short of money and the contractors agreed to recover their costs from the tenants' rents. These cottages had outside coalhouses, lavatories and wash houses which, by working-class standards of the mid-nineteenth century, were utopian. The railways were important customers of the brickmakers but the heavy tax on bricks, which was not abolished until 1850, forced them to use stone wherever possible.

The Industrial Revolution saw the start

production was here to stay. This new uniform brick was cheap and the old local brickworks could not compete; even stone districts succumbed to its use, particularly in the manufacturing towns and colliery villages of the north. Areas like Cumbria and the Cotswolds which had no industrial resources were protected and continued to use traditional materials. But elsewhere any semblance of a regional style was virtually eliminated by the late nineteenth century, with the increasing size of development, the closer control imposed by the Public Health Acts and, of course, the ever-increasing use of railway-borne materials.

Railway station and related outbuildings and cottages were built in a similar style. This is the Scottish baronial style station built in 1882 at Helen's Bay, County Down, Ireland.

of the large-scale production of bricks, tiles and slates. The first Welsh slate reached London by sea. Soon advantage was taken of the new canals to carry slate to inland towns. By the middle of the nineteenth century the railways carried the material all over the country. In the 1850s and 1860s the hand processing of bricks was mechanized. With the invention of the Hoffmann Kiln in 1858 the fires could burn continuously and mass

Typical railway cottage of the mid-nineteenth century

Industry

For the worker in the tin mines of Cornwall or the lead mines of Derbyshire mining and farming formed a twofold economy. It was the same in the uplands of West Yorkshire where farming was combined with weaving.

The cloth trade began to expand in the late seventeenth century and many clothiers, not wishing to disrupt family life too much, converted the kitchen into a workshop and then built a kitchen extension at the rear of their domestic quarters. Such early adaptations were made in rural areas.

Arkwright's water frame (1769), Hargreaves' spinning jenny, invented in 1764 and patented in 1770, and Crompton's spinning mule (1779) revolutionized the production of yarn and brought to the weaver an age of golden prosperity which was to last for a quarter of a century. But it was the loom and not the cotton mill that attracted immigrants in their thousands. The old loom shops could not cope, so new weavers' cottages with loom shops were built. These cottages, usually built of millstone grit, had a long range of windows on the upper floor to let in the maximum light. The space was unobstructed; there was good provision for storage and access for goods and workers. In some existing houses the roof was converted into a weaving loft or a two-storey workshop might be added. For many, small-scale farming, vegetable gardening, harvest work, etc., provided supplementary earnings. The growing population of the clothing towns of North and West Yorkshire demanded much more beef and butter than local

Late-eighteenth-century weaver's cottage

farms could produce and this market produced a new prosperity for the farmers who could now afford new building. Hilltop villages, like Hepstonstall, high above Hebden Bridge, have rows of weavers' cottages. With the invention of the power loom driven by water the domestic workshop was replaced by a factory in the valley and a town quickly developed around it.

The ending of the French wars created mass unemployment. Refugees fled to the blast furnaces, cotton mills and coal mines of the industrial north. While the non-industrialized communities of East Anglia and southeast England continued to build the traditional cottages, the urban industrial worker was crammed into terraced cottages or the notorious rows of back-to-back housing. Tiny inside, these two-storey, two-room houses were joined at the back by another. They lacked through ventilation. A row of ten houses would be separated from another by a courtyard where there was a pump and toilet serving the two rows.

The invention of the steam engine and the easy transportation of coal made any site suitable for factories and mills, which now sprawled over the valleys and hills congested by workers' housing. Poor or non-existent drainage produced appalling insanitary conditions. The Public Health Act (1875) attempted to end these slums.

Port Sunlight Estate, begun in 1888 at Wirral, Cheshire, was with Bournville, one of the earliest experiments in applying garden suburb ideas to the industrial scene. It was built for the workers at W. H. Levers Soapworks.

Terrace housing, Port Sunlight

Terrace in brick and half-timber, Port Sunlight

Block of nine cottages, Port Sunlight

Early industrial housing was not as revolutionary as that of the larger estates. Mostly there were small rows of cottages. In the 1770s the port of Whitehaven in Cumbria was designed by the Adam Brothers for Sir James Lowther. Its grand-scale architecture for the peasant cottage struck a slightly incongruous note. There were other schemes; the most visionary was Tremadoc (1816), in Gwynedd, by William Madocks, but he went bankrupt before it was realized. Some industrialists recognized the importance of well-housed, contented workers. At Barrow Bridge (1830), Lancashire, particular attention was paid to the attractive layout of the terraces. Here the cotton-textile workers were housed in five terraces, each of six houses, situated on a slope and surrounded by garden. The first major development providing an example of the more radical of utopian ideas was the industrial community of Saltaire, in West Yorkshire, begun in the 1860s. Here the building was influenced by the Italian Renaissance. In the 1890s George Cadbury developed Bournville near Birmingham, and Lord Leverhulme built Port Sunlight in Merseyside for employees of the Lever factory. Both were pioneer developments and both tried to break down the distinction between housing for the worker and housing for others. At Port Sunlight it was done with a middle-class disguise but both eventually became models for the future suburbia.

The result of the garden suburb experiments at Bournville and Port Sunlight had a profound affect on later developments. An obvious influence was on Hampstead Garden Suburb, begun in 1906.

Terrace housing designed by Louis de Soissons at Welwyn Garden City, Hertfordshire. Work on the Garden City was begun in 1920.

The Picturesque

Many cottages in the late eighteenth century were insanitary and had become dilapidated. Some landlords found it amusing to rebuild them in a picturesque manner, and by the 1780s numerous pattern books provided appropriate examples. Variety was most important and irregular walls, projecting eaves, gabled ends and porches with elaborate barge boards over the gable roofs were built. Sir Uvedale Price's *Essays on the Picturesque* (1794), full of nostalgia for the romantic Virgilian scene, did much to establish the cult.

Some landlords had already found the villages near the manor houses too obtrusive. When Lord Dorchester enlarged the abbey at Milton Abbas in Dorset in 1750 he demolished the village and later laid out a new one further away. Symmetrically-grouped cottages, each separated by a plot of land, lined a long street. There were other schemes, at Harewood in West Yorkshire, and Lowther in Cumbria, each conceived as an improvement to the approaches to a Great House. These new villages were considered appropriate settings for the besmocked rustics. J. B. Papworth, who was responsible for much of the best architecture in Cheltenham between 1800 and 1840, saw advantages in designing picturesque houses for the labouring poor. But he felt any symbols of ease and luxury should be omitted as they would 'ill associate with the modest and moderate claims of this respectable and useful class of society'.

The eighteenth-century concept of landscape as an extension of the architecture was abandoned and the village was considered as a related and picturesque part of the landscape. The cottage *ornée*, popularized by the Royal Lodge in Windsor Great Park (1814), was a picturesque villa that aped the small-scale traditional buildings with its thatch and fancy detailing. Pseudo-Gothic chapter houses built as lodges and casemented keepers' cottages began to appear. The richer landlords throughout the nineteenth century took great pleasure in this sort of building. Many of the books did, however, deal with cheap, practical and well-built housing. John Plaw who was partly responsible for the development of Southampton published *Ferme Ornée or Rural Improvements* in 1795. He preferred the rational and commonsense to the picturesque solution for rehousing labourers on an estate.

During the early nineteenth century a large proportion of villages were built according to picturesque principles. Most were modelled on Blaise Hamlet, in Avon, which was built in 1810–12 by the

Model cottages designed by George Dance in 1806 at East Stratton, Hampshire

*A typical romanticized estate cottage at
Sudbourne, Suffolk*

Quaker banker, J. S. Harford. Blaise
Hamlet is a combination of nostalgia and
cliché. Harford's architect was John
Nash who worked in association with
George Repton. Blaise, unlike earlier
examples which replaced a destroyed
village, was new. Variety in plan and style
was considered essential; for example the
pantry and cellar are more obvious in the

cottages here than in cottages at Nuneham Courtenay (1760), Oxforshire,
where they were hidden for reasons of
symmetry. Later the village concept was
extended and villages such as Harlaxton
(1831) in Lincolnshire which originally
consisted of a core of older cottages grew
as new cottages in the same style
were built.

Cottages designed by John Nash at Blaise Hamlet near Westbury-on-Trym, Avon

Charles Rennie Mackintosh and C. F. A. Voysey are two of the few architects of the turn of this century who understood traditional buildings and the possibilities of creating a new architecture by the rearrangement of traditional plans and methods.
The Orchards, Chorley Wood, Hertfordshire, designed by Voysey between 1898 and 1899.

The misuse of traditional plans this century is highlighted by this L.C.C. Estate at Becontree, Greater London, built between 1920 and 1930.

The scale is exaggeratedly large; the traditional elements are applied as a cosmetic.

79

Design by Voysey for The Cottage, Bishop's Itchington, Warwickshire, 1888–9. Voysey (1857–1941) was perhaps the least committed of theoreticians but one of the most gifted artists. His designs are precise, bold and simple with a freshness and freedom from stylistic imitation which detached them from other architects' designs treading a similar direction.

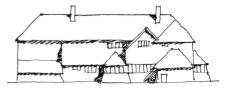

Windy Hill House, Kilmacolm, near Glasgow, designed in 1899 by Charles Rennie Mackintosh. The material used was a local grey sandstone clad with a traditional grey finishing material. With its steeply-pitched roofs, smooth walls and windows cut simply into them, it differs only slightly from the traditional Scottish farmhouse in the freedom of plan and the total integration of interior design. The building had considerable influence on Continental architecture, particularly the works of Olbrich and Hoffmann.

The Dunes, an early range of cottages built at Thorpeness, Suffolk, between 1911 and 1914. Notice the use of close studding, the status symbol of the wealthy and fashionable in the Middle Ages, as a cosmetic to the building.

The Future Cottage

The cottage is the picturesque idyll for many people; but for the radicals, bent on an efficient mass-produced substitute, preservation of the outworn and antique is reactionary twaddle. There are others, however, who have different reasons for favouring the cottage. From the eighteenth century onwards, particularly after the Jacobite rebellion, village building was taken up with missionary zeal by

A typical house in Gloucestershire. As in the nineteenth century, the twentieth century continues to romanticize the house and cottage.

landowners and reformers. As far as they were concerned the only way to turn the Scots into a productive and amenable body was to develop an ordered pattern of settlement which would also form the framework for a stabilized economy. But there were ulterior motives. Once repentent and sufficiently servile the Scots and the Irish would provide a supply of labour to be exploited by the capitalists.

It was an equally attractive proposition for the nineteenth-century landowner to provide a tied cottage and if it was not to keep his labour force then it was, as far as he was concerned, simply an amusing idea to build rustic cottages. The model villages built by Cadbury and Lever were, for the times, perhaps the most moral and

utopian, based on progressive ideas and advanced planning. But the building designs either aped the currently fashionable style or through a drab middle-class disguise, heralded the future suburbia. But all this is far removed from the shanty erected at night on the common. Today these are seen only in the handmade houses of America or the shanties found outside the new cities in the Third World. Here buildings are made the traditional way, from materials at hand; today these materials are society's waste salvaged from the rubbish dumps and junkyards.

The cottage proper has been taken over by the architect and speculative builder. Few seem to know what it is about. Le Corbusier took a great interest in primi-

Well Hall, the munitions estate built at Eltham in Kent during this century, took the gabled dormer of the Gloucestershire cottage (see page 81) as a characteristic feature, but

then distorted it in scale and texture. This, in its own way, became a model for other vernacular revival schemes.

tive societies and out of this interest sprang a series of buildings constructed in a modern folk style. The houses made use of very simple materials ready to hand such as rough stone, fair-faced brick, raw concrete or unfinished timber. This was a continuation of the utilitarian tradition of the cottager. He looked at primitive man not for his barbarity but for his wisdom. It was this wisdom that Le Corbusier hoped the new buildings would revive. In the 1950s James Stirling, and other architects of the English *avant-garde*, turned with increasing interest to the traditional buildings of Britain's Industrial Revolution. This was not out of nostalgia but out of an admiration for the functional and utilitarian nature of such buildings. Their projects were not simply a stripped-down version of the picturesque, but a contribution to the tradition of the cottager's building art. They understood the language of this art and adjusted it to a twentieth-century grammar. Everything about the cottager and his cottage was there to be seen. But for many others there are ulterior motives: the pattern books have been brought back and ahead lies a veneer of mock-Tudor to be exploited by those who care little for the traditional building methods and understand even less about the traditional cottage form. There is a strong tradition behind the construction and form of the cottage, a tradition the fakes on many of the suburban housing estates misunderstand. Because there was a village and work in the local fields, mines or quarries a simple hut or cottage was built. It had little or no pretentions. It was an honest answer to basic needs. Today we see the cottage through different eyes. To many it has become a delightful *bijou* residence. But perhaps it is this new way of seeing the cottage that is the main reason for the fakes of today.

A project for mass housing at Lima, Peru, 1969, by James Stirling. The project is a radical alternative of the vernacular revival schemes offered by most architects. Here the architect provided a basic structure which was later to be developed by the occupant. The project is a combination of architecture and vernacular building.

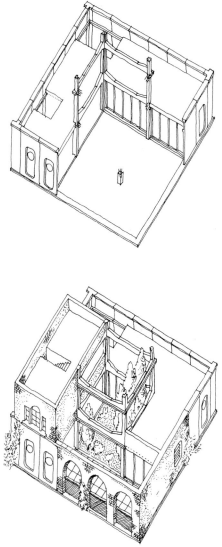

The West Country

Society, which made Bath both rich and famous, brought to the West Country a classical spirit of a scale and dignity which made this city the epitome of eighteenth-century urbanism. But it was the belt of limestone that gave this area its characteristic buildings. It provided the well-drained pastureland for sheep and cattle, and the consequent development of the woollen and clothing industries produced the wealth to quarry the limestone which was used for building. The great hills, like the Quantocks and the Brendon Hills, were, and still are, sheep country.

Devon's prosperity was based on the export of serges woven on its cottage looms and cleansed and thickened, or fulled, in small tucking mills on the rapid streams of Dartmoor. And, of course, busy ports such as Brixham, where William of Orange landed in 1688, Dartmouth which was the assembly point for the Second and Third Crusades in 1147 and 1190, and Plymouth, the embarkation point of the Pilgrim Fathers to the New World in 1620, were crucial to this trade. The woollen industry flourished from the Middle Ages until the end

Previous page. *The Old Post Office at Tintagel, Cornwall. Note the massive stepped chimney stack sited in the front wall of the main room rather than the transverse wall. This is characteristic of the West Country.*

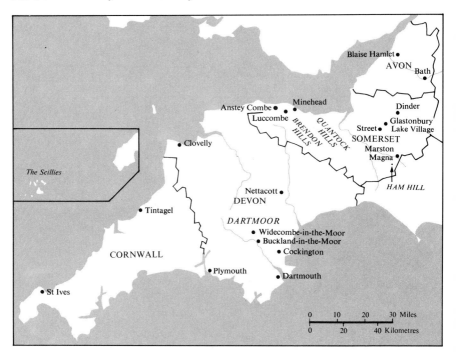

of the eighteenth century, bringing prosperity and wealth. An example of this wealth is reflected in the beautifully carved rood-screens found in the fifteenth-and sixteenth-century churches of Devon.

Man has lived on Dartmoor since the Bronze Age. In those days it was drier and settled by farming and pastoral communities. They lived in circular stone huts of low walls some three to four feet in thickness. The turf or thatch roofs were supported by timber rafters which rose to a point. These huts were usually surrounded by walled enclosures called pounds. A wetter phase drove much of the population away. But the tin in the Devon valleys made the area one of the most important sources of this mineral in twelfth-century Europe. The miners who

came to work in the valleys pushed the remaining farmers to settle on the stonier uplands.

It was not until the thirteenth century that the Moor was again colonized. Houses were long and narrow and invariably built on a gentle slope. The family lived at one end, with the cattle under the same roof at the lower end so that the slurry could be drained away down the hill. The fireplace was an open hearth. A characteristic feature is the local granite used in the construction of the house. This was the beginning of the traditional longhouse.

The major building boom in Devon occurred during the seventeenth century when the area was extensively settled following the defeat of the Armada in 1588. Timber-framed buildings were rare,

A view of Bath, the epitome of eighteenth-century urbanism

much of the timber being reserved for roofs and floor joists while the bulk went into the construction of the ships for the English fleet.

The typical cottage during the Middle Ages was built of mud mixed with straw or stubble to bind the material together. This type of walling, known as cob, survives largely in the southwestern counties, particularly Devon. The cob was thrown on to the wall and then trodden down and left to dry in the sun. The walling was slowly built up in layers over several months. Windows, door frames and floor joists were built into the walling at the same time. There was no supporting timber frame to the wall. The cob walls were often built on a low stone foundation over which they projected an inch or so as protection against vermin and damp. The corners of the houses were generally rounded off to avoid cracking, the most common weakness of cob walling. Walls were whitewashed or colour-washed, and the normal roofing material was a cover of thatch.

The usual method of applying thatch was to pin it down with rods and broaches. But in some of the more primitive houses of Cornwall, as in the Isle of Man, the thatch was heaped into a dome shape, criss-crossed with ropes made of straw or some other material to prevent it being blown off bodily by the gales. These ropes were either tied to projecting pieces of slate pegged to the walls or weighted down at their ends by rocks. Similar methods were used on the Atlantic coast of Ireland and in the Western Highlands.

The major innovation in the late sixteenth century was the introduction of

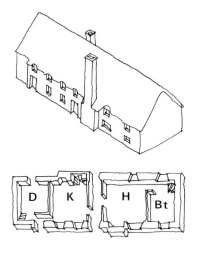

Plan and view of a cob-built yeoman house of the early Stuart period at Nettacott, Upton Pyne, Devon.

the cross passage. The farmer was more interested in cattle than sheep or corn and needed frequent access from the dairy to the yard at the rear of the house. A passage across the house was the natural solution. The dairy by this time was a common feature in most farmhouses throughout the western half of England from Lancashire to Devon.

The longhouse was still to be found on the edges of Dartmoor in the late sixteenth century. There had always been access across the house between the living quarters and the byre. The process of separating the two began with a partition forming a cross passage between the two. The origins of many cross passages was not as a passage within the hall for domestic use, but as a passage taking the cattle into the byre. In Devon and

Left. *Whitewashed cob and thatched cottages at Luccombe, Somerset*

Somerset the cross passage is usually wider than many found elsewhere in England, often six to seven feet in width. Fireplaces were positioned against the wall of the passage. When the hall was chambered over, the staircase was built not, as was the usual rule, against the fireplace as a newel or spiral staircase, but on the back wall in its own projection of stone or cob, as in the farmhouses of Guernsey and Jersey.

In the early seventeenth century the yeoman farmer adopted an idea from the larger houses and built a chimney stack on the front wall which served both hall and chamber. The longhouse type of building persisted, but increasingly the cattle were kept in a separate shippon. The partition walls of the early cross passage were gradually replaced by a stone wall. The passage was now part of the house proper and used purely for domestic purposes. A chamber was often built over it. By the mid-seventeenth century many farms had a gabled porch with a wool store built over the entrance.

The growing demand for fresh bread resulted in the bread oven which bulges out from the walls of many small seventeenth-century houses in Devon. Another Devonshire characteristic is the smoking chamber for smoking bacon. This was built in the gable end beside the fireplace and consists of a chamber with an opening at a lower level from the fireplace. It has a corbelled, or projecting, roof with a flue connected to the main chimney. Another improvement was the cream oven which was found in the hall away from the fireplace, and was used for scalding cream to make it clot.

Many of the smaller buildings in the mountain and moorland districts such as Dartmoor, the Isle of Man, North Wales

Developments of the Dartmoor longhouse:

The simplest type with one single entry and cross walk for use by both man and beast. There is no division between shippon and cross walk.

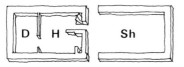

A wooden partition separates the shippon from the cross walk which now becomes a cross passage.

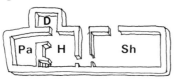

By the mid-seventeenth century a stone wall replaced the wooden partition and a separate entrance was opened into the shippon. Shippon and the main house were connected by a door leading off the cross passage.

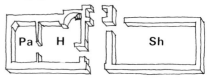

By the early eighteenth century the separation between shippon and the main house becomes more distinct. The house itself is radically enlarged.

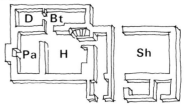

and the Scottish Highlands, were built of unquarried stone. In Cornwall, for example blocks of granite were used producing a simple but solid building. The walls were usually two feet or more in thickness. Often the stones were bedded in earth and then plastered or whitewashed over. Gaps between the boulders were filled with small stones or rubble. Few builders were able to construct roofs to span more than one room across and so plans were enlarged by adding on additional bays, by an outshut or by a right-angled projection.

Cottages built of a local quarried stone had thinner walls, between eighteen inches and two feet thick, the internal cavity being filled with rubble or small stones. A characteristic of houses in Cornwall and on Dartmoor is the tall tapering chimney. The cottages of Cornwall and Devon are also known for their gardens. Flowers abound in the temperate climate and produce a blaze of colour.

A common feature of stone houses in late-seventeenth-century Somerset was the storeyed bay window. It was built on to the hall or parlour and allowed additional light into a room. It also gave people a chance to see what was going on

By the late seventeenth century the Devonshire longhouse had incorporated separate doorways leading into the cross passage and byre. This longhouse is near Widecombe-in-the-Moor.

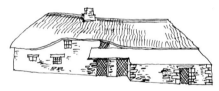

A small house serving as a farm building at Nettacott, Upton Pyne, Devon, built in the mid-seventeenth century. The cross passage was later closed and the end turned into a larder. Note the oven built out from the main hall beside the fire.

A common type of house plan, found in the Ham Hill area of Somerset from the sixteenth century until the early eighteenth century, consisted of a hall with a parlour partitioned off at the end. A kitchen at the other end was separated from the main living room by a cross passage behind the fireplace. Beside the entrance door from the passage to the living room a staircase leads to the bedrooms. Windows in the gable end give additional light, while the principal bedroom has a dormer window.

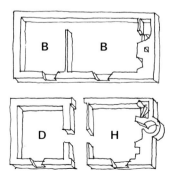

up and down the street. By now house interiors had become more fashionable. Ornamental plasterwork, confined originally to the Great House, was sometimes seen decorating the ceiling and walls of the smaller houses.

The double house, consisting of two one-room-deep ranges planned side by side, began to make an appearance. Rarely were roofs spanning more than eighteen feet attempted and each range had its own pitch roof built parallel to the other with a lead valley in between. The increased size in plan lead to an inevitable change in the use of the room. The hall, which was no longer used for cooking, was thought of as a parlour while the new kitchen was used both as a cooking room and a dining room.

As early as the thirteenth century, stone slates had replaced thatch for roofing in the large towns, but now stone slate was increasingly used as a roof covering in the countryside as well. In the eastern part of Somerset pantiles are a characteristic roof covering.

Engineering developments such as James Watt's invention for draining the mines (1777) and Humphry Davy's invention of a miner's safety lamp (1815)

encouraged mining to such an extent that, by the nineteenth century, Cornwall was producing two-thirds of the world's supply of copper. The miners were housed in small detached cottages or cottage rows, a development of the longhouse, consisting of two storeys with one or two rooms on each floor.

The period from 1750 to 1880 saw a rise in population and farmers were confronted with unprecedented demands not only for food, but also for raw materials and feed for draught animals such as horses and oxen. The gathering of land into large estates, the movement to an optimum size of farms, and the growth of mixed grain farming and animal husbandry were reaching their climax. River navigations, turnpikes and canals were improved to meet the pressing need for easier transport of agricultural products and building materials for the immense rebuilding programme that was taking place in towns and villages stimulated by an expanding population and changing agriculture. Such a pressing building programme was bound to surface in the current cottage *ornée* style or the fashionable model village of picturesque villas of the late eighteenth and nineteenth centuries. The most famous was Blaise Hamlet, Avon, built in 1810. Many cottage *ornées* had been built and although Sir Uvedale Price's manifesto, *Essays on the Picturesque*, had been published some twenty years before, this was the first attempt to group them into a village. The village was built by John Nash and George Repton for the Quaker banker, J. S. Harford. The nine cottages, built to house the elderly employees of

Houses at Dinder, Somerset, showing the characteristic gabled dormer

Right. A cottage at Blaise Hamlet. Note the elegant Tudoresque chimney.

Blaise Castle, were grouped around a green. The architects considered variety between the cottages was essential and inspiration was taken from literature and painting rather than from the traditional or vernacular buildings.

Other villages were built: Street, in Somerset, was a model factory village built in 1829 by the Quaker leather manufacturers, Clarks; Hasletown, in Cornwall, an early nineteenth-century tin-mining village, consisted of sturdy stone-built cottages each with their own cottage garden. The designs by this time were simpler.

As the twentieth century approached architects began to look more closely at the traditional cottage style. The result was a more utilitarian and austere style culminating in the cottage designs by C. F. Voysey for Lord Lovelace at Anstey Combe, in Somerset, in 1936. But the builder continued to put on the pitched roofs and to introduce rustic irregularity.

A thatched cottage at Blaise Hamlet, near Westbury-on-Trym, Avon. Only three cottages were thatched, the others were tiled.

Right. *Cob cottages at Minehead, Somerset*

94

Cottages lining the cobbled street in Clovelly, Devon

By the mid 1960s the architect, more for change than for any logical reason, turned his hand to the arrangement of suburban housing estates along picturesque lines. There was an assumption, at Blaise Hamlet at least, that people wanted, metaphorically speaking, to escape, and that variety and nostalgia were the passwords. Nash was far too intelligent to imagine that external ornamentation would transport people into some kind of utopian dream world, but the mistake today is that these ideas are inclined to be taken far too seriously. The cottage *ornée* is taken as the real cottage, and the real cottage is regarded as a poor substitute. The style of the cottage *ornée* was simply a joke, sometimes in bad taste, but many people were not only hard of hearing but also short-sighted as well. The dream, knocked off its Virgilian pedestal sank rapidly into the banalities of suburbia. But today the stone and cob cottages in the villages of Devon and Cornwall survive to remind us of the past. The hamlets and fishing villages such as Clovelly and Cockington attract thousands of visitors each year who delight in the traditional thatched cottages. Perhaps the twentieth-century architect and builder in providing the picturesque is simply answering the demands that imply a return of the traditional, but the fake traditional that many produce is surely not the answer?

Right. *Cottages at Burford, Oxfordshire.*
The lintels to the windows and door openings are of timber.

The Southern Counties
and the Channel Isles

Southern England is essentially an agricultural area, although Portsmouth has been a chief seaport of the Royal Navy since the reign of Henry VII, and Southampton which has been the ocean-liner base for the last hundred years, was the embarkation port for soldiers leaving to fight in the Crusades and the French wars during the Middle Ages. It was at Southampton that the Saxons under Cerdic landed in A.D. 495 and founded the kingdom of Wessex. It has always been an important commercial port; during the

fifteenth century exports included wool, cloth, tin, lead and hides and major imports included fine armour, spices, drugs, oriental silks, cotton, sweet wines and sugar. Many of these imports were carried by Venetian ships which used Southampton as their main port of call until the sixteenth century. This is the area of the Great Houses such as Wilton House, Stourhead, Bramshill House and Longleat. But it also has a strong rustic tradition. Thomas Hardy wrote about this rustic tradition in his novels based on

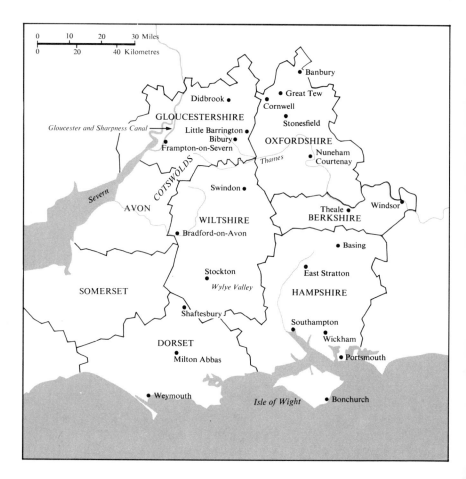

country life in the southern and western counties of England.

The fourteenth-century tithe barn at Bradford-on-Avon in Wiltshire gives some indication of how Saxon chieftains and landowners lived. Until the Middle Ages churches, barns and residences of leaders were similar in construction. Many were built of timber but some, like the tithe barn at Bradford-on-Avon, were built of stone. The roof was made of open timber framing. The windows were generally small and provided ventilation. The hearth was in the centre of the building, the smoke escaping through holes in the roof. It was in the hall that the chief would live with his family, servants and fighting men. The walls would be decorated with shields and antlers, while the earthen floor would be covered with rushes. Oxen were housed in stalls at the lower end of the hall. Around the hall would be grouped the wooden church, sleeping quarters, store rooms and the kitchen. Nearby would be the hovels of the villagers; they were usually built of branches, walled with mud, and roofed with thatch or turf. The chimneys were simply holes in the roofs.

But under the ambitious land-hungry Marcher Barons of the twelfth century the Cotswolds were turned into a prosperous countryside with a land cropped and harvested, and valleys thick with corn. It was on the foundations laid at this time that Cotswold wool became one of the richest commodities in the world.

By the fourteenth century England had a population of about $3\frac{3}{4}$ million. The Black Death, which entered Britain at Melcombe Regis, now part of Weymouth, in 1348, killed one-third of the population. It accelerated the decline of feudalism since labour shortages increased the cost of labour. Under feudalism serfs worked forty days a year on the lord's land without payment. Now pressure increased for the lord to commute the services on the land for a money wage thus making the serf a freeman.

Today this whole area is defined by the limestone belt that runs diagonally from Dorset to Lincolnshire, but despite the ready supply of loose stone, which probably exceeded that of timber, particularly in the Cotswolds, it was rarely used for cottage building until the late sixteenth century. The characteristic housing in the Banbury region of Oxfordshire in the sixteenth century had adopted the cruck-frame method of roofing by raising the cruck blades several feet off the

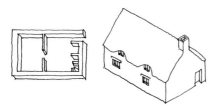

Typical small houses in the southern part of the limestone belt of the Cotswolds. The entrance planned at the gable end is typical until the early eighteenth century. The smallest plan probably had a ladder to the loft.

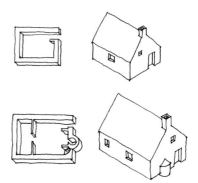

ground and resting them in walls up to 2 feet 8 inches in thickness. New building was still in the medieval tradition of a rectangular plan, one room deep. Occasionally a cross wing would be added.

Many timber houses had the filling between the timber posts plastered flush and painted white or colour-washed. Brick nogging was often used, but on the border where Berkshire, Wiltshire and Hampshire meet, a filling occurs of alternate layers of brick and flint. Most of these houses were roofed with thatch. Timber building was rare towards the west, in Dorset, where cob walling, and occasionally stone, with a thatch roof was more common. The cob cottages of

Dorset were built with chalk mixed with clay, and straw was used to bind the mixture together, but in the sandy districts heather was used instead. The walling was then built up in layers of two to three feet high and two feet in thickness, each layer being left to settle for a day or two before another was added. But cob walling was laborious and the structural limitations it imposed restricted its use almost entirely to buildings of humbler status like the small farmhouse and cottage. Most cottages in the late seventeenth century consisted of one or two rooms. Few had storage space, larders or sculleries. The bake-oven was generally built into the wall beside the

A large farmhouse in West Gloucestershire – a Tudor manor house built more like a town house. The roomy garrets in the jettied and gabled second floor were used for storing produce.

The one-cell Cotswold cottage. Storage area and small parlour were partitioned off from the main room. A feature of the interior is the compactness.

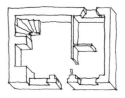

Cottage at Stockton built of Wiltshire limestone. Note the bake-oven projecting out of the front wall.

The two-cell Cotswold cottage. The bake-oven was usually incorporated as shown, opening out of the fireplace in the kitchen.

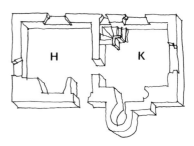

Above. *Picturesque planting by J. C. Loudon at Great Tew near Banbury in Oxfordshire*

Below. *A stone-built cottage with a thatched roof in Dorset at East Lulworth. This cottage has a through passage behind the chimney stack and a service room beyond.*

fireplace which was usually very large in comparison to the room. An enormous brick or plastered funnel projected into the room and this was often so unstable that it was replaced by bringing the whole chimney-breast forward. Occasionally stone seats were hollowed out of the walls on either side of the fireplace. The early cottage staircase was a steep ladder, but this was replaced by a compact staircase built around a central newel or pillar and it was usually positioned in a corner by the chimney. Many floors were plastered by packing clay on wattle and laid between the joists, while red bricks, tiles or stone flags were used for the ground floors. Timber and stone buildings are seldom seen in the heart of a stone-producing area and they are usually found only in areas such as Gloucestershire which lies between the stone uplands and the timber plain. Quite simply, if stone was available the cottager would use it.

Between 1580 and 1690 the prosperity of the cloth industry on the Severn side of the Cotswolds combined with the abundance of building materials turned Oxfordshire and Gloucestershire into a building world of their own. The major differences were in the richness and quality of detailing as limestone was quarried not only for the manor houses and market halls but also for the humblest cottages. The limestone gives the houses a warm mellow appearance even when it has matured with time to a deep grey colour.

The dormer window, a product of the Middle Ages for making headroom in the roof space, was turned into one of the most characteristic features of the Cotswolds with the gabled dormer flush with the façades of the house. A third room called the backhouse or netherhouse was added to the hall and parlour of the

Characteristic detached Cotswold cottage at Little Barrington, Gloucestershire. The most characteristic feature is the gabled dormer window and finished, like the gable walls, with carved finials, copings, decorative kneelers or stone-slate verges.

farmhouse often in an outshut under a lean-to roof. It was a general-purpose service room which gradually began to take on the function of kitchen or milkhouse. Chimneys were built either at the gabled end or in the centre of the house, and the use of stone made them both massive and simple, and limited the stacks to rectangular or square plans.

Unlike Yorkshire and the north, large blocks of stone were rare in the south, consequently any large stones were reserved for window-dressings and quoins, while random rubble was used for most cottage walls. Windows were composed of lights formed by the division of window openings by mullions. The lights themselves were often made of wrought-iron casements separated by moulded stone mullions. The lights to ground-floor windows were usually more numerous than those of the first-floor or dormer windows. Above the head and

Right. Arlington Row, Bibury, Gloucestershire. The stone-tiled roofs and gabled dormers are typical of this area.

returns to openings for both windows and doors was a drip-moulding built to divert rainwater away from the openings – another characteristic detail of Cotswold building. There is much ornamental detailing to be seen in the Cotswolds in the mouldings of doorways and windows and in the carvings of finials of roofs and gables. In humbler dwellings timber window frames and doorheads were used instead of stone. Cottages lining the village street very occasionally had a bay

window which was a flat rather than a round projection, and often incorporated the front door under the same stone-slated roof.

In the Channel Islands the hall house consisted of one large room, the hall, and a smaller room, the buttery. By the late seventeenth century lofts were being installed and the two-storey house, built first in the sixteenth century, was now becoming common. Walls were usually two to three feet thick. They were built of

Rows of cottages, Broadway, Hereford and Worcester, showing the combined roof for both the entrance door and bay window.

Typical large parlour, two-storey farmhouse of the early eighteenth century. Note the staircase, built in a tower projecting at the rear of the house.

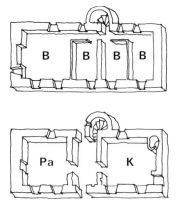

Bay windows were rarely used in cottages. They are usually found as a flat projection beside a door to the street. Sometimes the bay might be built two storeys high with a dormer gable. A characteristic is the single ground-floor bay combined with the street door under the same stone-slated hood.

External staircase tower, Guernsey. The tower is called a tourelle and encloses a stone staircase, in this case circular, but sometimes square.

two faces of masonry, the space between being filled with clay mortar and quarry rubble. Windows in the sixteenth and seventeenth centuries were very small, and were usually splayed on the inside but many were enlarged after 1600. Fireplaces were quite elaborate, the hood being carried on decorated stone lintels and projecting brackets called corbels. Many farmhouses had circular stone staircases enclosed in a tower known as a tourelle which were being built well into the eighteenth century. Others had a straight staircase built externally.

But the pioneering model villages of Milton Abbas in Dorset and Nuneham Courtenay in Oxfordshire had already been built by the late eighteenth century. Nuneham Courtenay, the best-known model village, was built to replace the old village of Newham Courtenay. It was built by Lord Harcourt, and consisted of nineteen pairs of red-brick cottages, one-and-a-half storeys high, with dormers in the roof. Milton Abbas replaced the destroyed market town which stood in Lord Milton's park. The building began in 1773 with Capability Brown as the landscape architect and Sir William Chambers was the planner. Similar villages were built in Britain throughout the nineteenth century.

Milton Abbas, the model village built by Lord Dorchester in the late eighteenth century in Dorset. Note the simplicity and regularity of the design.

The rustic cottage came into its own at this time. J. B. Papworth, one of the architects of Cheltenham, published a book entitled *Rural Residences* in 1818 which discussed the advantages of more picturesque houses for the labouring poor. He felt that too much ornament was immodest, but he was not against adapting the cottage to park scenery, and the result was the cottage *ornée*. In 1865 a modification of the Poor Law, which spread the poor rate over the whole district instead of a single parish, encouraged the larger owners to build and by the 1880s housing conditions had greatly improved. Ideas in building became more utilitarian. By 1900 a full circle had turned.

One of the last model villages to be built was Cornwell in Oxfordshire. It is a village of picture-book prettiness nestling in a fold of hills and consists of reconstructed cottages in Cotswold stone built by Clough Williams-Ellis in 1930. It continued, as many estates do to this day, the bogus picturesqueness of the Virgilian scene. The sad thing about such picturesque ideas was that the model they used was not the *real* village but the cosmetic picturesqueness idealized in eighteenth- and nineteenth-century watercolours and twentieth-century picture postcards. Such notions were adopted, as they are to this day, as some sort of panacea for the ills of society. The diversity of the street lines, the irregularity of wall heights and the variety of rustic textures were intended to make life more pleasant. But this happened only in the *closed* village owned by the local lord who would have restricted the type of building. The lessons to be learned from the older established *open* village settlements had been ignored.

The characteristic feature of the early farmhouses of Guernsey and Jersey is the

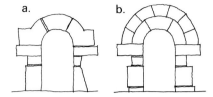

a. *Typical Jersey arch*
b. *Typical Guernsey arch*
One of the most striking features of the Guernsey and Jersey farmhouse is the semi-circular arched doorway. These arched doorways were unknown in the Channel Islands before the Reformation. They were most likely developed by some of the Huguenot refugees, especially as arched doorways were common in the Avranches district in southwest Normandy and North Brittany. No arches older than 1570 are known, and the arch finally went out of favour during the Civil War. Each island has developed its own distinct style. In Guernsey the round-arch doorway usually has the arch in two voussoirs or semi-circular rows of stones, which are shoulders. In Jersey, the arch often has one row of stones only, and the springer stones (the first stones laid in an arch) have 'L' shaped shoulders and are generally less massive than Guernsey arches.

round arch. Those in Guernsey are larger than those in Jersey. The obvious French influence is probably explained by the flood of Huguenot refugees who entered the islands following the massacre of St Bartholomew (1572). Another common feature found in the oldest houses, both large and small, is the niche in the stone wall beside the door, probably a development of the ancient Roman bathing basin known as a piscina, it may well have contained water or possibly a lantern.

The seventeenth-century cottages of Dorset are usually more utilitarian and austere than those of the Tudor period. Some roofs were slated with large grey stones, but thatch was the most typical roof covering. Roof pitches are shallower than those of southeast England, the

A cottage interior, Wiltshire

Midlands and the north. Many have hipped roofs with sloping rather than gabled ends. The thatch is scalloped around small dormers or carried in a catilide over a rough outshut. The thatch, usually straw, was applied by pinning it down with a system of rods and broaches which is the most usual way of working in England. The Romans had roofed their buildings with stone slates nailed to battens but here the stone slates were fixed by an oaken peg. They were laid to a low pitch, about thirty degrees, and diminished in size towards the ridge. The stone slates were cleverly worked around valleys, avoiding the use of lead or tiles.

In some areas stone was combined with flint in decorative banding. This was a common feature of houses built on the chalk uplands of Dorset from the mid-seventeenth century onwards. Cottages built of rough stone usually found at random on the ground nearby are typical of Wiltshire, parts of Hampshire, Dorset and Berkshire. This rough stone is called pudding stone, and provided a fairly

107

unpretentious looking material for building. Along the Dorset border with Wiltshire some walls are built of a combination of pudding stone, brick and flint. The walls were nearly always whitewashed.

The countryside in the traditional agricultural areas was changing rapidly. By the beginning of the eighteenth century much of the land had become heavily enclosed and the cottagers had become landless labourers. Life steadily became worse for the cottager. The combination of low wages, unemployment, bad-living conditions and inflation lay at the origins of outbreaks of violence culminating in the last Labourers' Revolt of 1830. Strangely it was not the more-recently-enclosed Midlands but the old-enclosed poverty-stricken counties of southern England in Kent, East and West Sussex, Dorset and Hampshire that were most troubled. The poorer cottages were still small and badly built. Many were built of mud with thatched roofs. There was usually one bedroom for the whole family, few had privies, and many floors were still made of clay or broken stone which became sodden when it rained. Few were lucky enough to live in the Gothic- or Tudor-style cottages erected by a great landlord.

A typical villa estate at Undercliff, Bonchurch on the Isle of Wight in 1837. By this time the cottage had become a holiday villa and the styles of building made reference to both the classical and the romantic, but the results were far removed from either.

London's Country and Coast

Fragments of woodland in the Kentish Weald, the Surrey commons and the remains of Ashdown Forest are all that is left of the once unbroken forest covering Kent, Sussex and Surrey in the Middle Ages. When Edward III made the journey from London to Rye in the mid-fourteenth century he had to employ no less than twenty-two guides. It was both a difficult and perilous journey, with the forests abounding in fox, wild cat and wolf, still formidable rivals to man. Here and there, settlers were cutting out denes in the forest where they could maintain a few animals and develop a primitive form of agriculture. The medieval cottage was a small one-room shanty with a central fire for cooking and heating. The smoke found its way out through small, unglazed openings. These openings were usually closed by wooden shutters or canvas blinds. Furniture and domestic vessels were scanty – a trestle table, some stools, a clothes chest, pots and pans,

Previous page. *A typical Kentish cottage and garden at Meopham*

earthenware pitchers and other rudimentary kitchen utensils. The women made their own coarse cloth and linen, they made candles, and stitched and stuffed sheepskin bags for cart saddles. The men tanned their own leather, made the farm implements and the simpler cottage furniture, while travelling carpenters, smiths and tinkers supplied the remaining hardware. When the weather was fine the women would cook outside.

The more prosperous households lived, dined and slept in one main hall. Sometimes the lord and his family might sleep and live in a separate room called the solar. It was a more comfortable room, containing chairs, tables, and an elaborate feather bed. The walls might be covered with tapestries and the floor with a woven rush mat. Often the windows were glazed.

Beneath the Wealden forest the soil was rich in iron ore. The indigenous oaks of the forest were cut down and roasted into charcoal for smelting the ore, while small primitive foundries supplied iron for the armour and weapons. This, for centuries, was the Black Country of England. But the growth of towns and villages, the construction of wooden ships and the ever-increasing clearances for agriculture so denuded the forests that a law was passed in the reign of Elizabeth I rationing the felling of oaks. The result was that timbers other than oak were used for building. Much was imported, the timbers used in the box-framed house were made thinner, the panelling between the timbers was made larger and squarer and gradually the timber-frame houses of the early Tudor period became more austere. The last iron foundry to close was at Lamberhurst, in Kent, in 1765. It was here that the railings round St Paul's Cathedral were forged. The great fortunes made by the ironmasters between the fifteenth and eighteenth centuries had already built some of the fine Wealden houses, matching the mansions of the medieval weavers.

The fourteenth century saw considerable changes in English life and society. After the Black Death (1348–9), the scarcity of labour and the profits to be

A cottage typical of late medieval Kent. The central chimney stack and fireplace would probably have been added in the seventeenth century. By the eighteenth century an attic with dormer windows would probably have been formed in the roof.

Timber-framed cottage at Eardisland, Hertfordshire. In the eighteenth century the roof was raised to give more headroom to the bedrooms.

made from wool resulted in an expansion of sheep farming. At the same time leasehold farming increased as landowners, unable to afford labour, broke their estates up into holdings which they stocked and let to rent. Edward III (1327–77), whose attempt to claim the

Synards, Otham, Kent. A Wealden type of house, built of timber in the late fifteenth century. It has a two-bay open hall and two-storeyed end bays. The timber framing is in close studding. In 1603 the attic was floored and the dormer window made.

Open hall house, typical of the southeast in the late fifteenth century. They were lofty halls usually built with two-storeyed ends and are particularly characteristic of Surrey, Kent, Essex and Suffolk. In most of these houses the passage was usually partitioned off from the main hall rather than within the service rooms on either side of the central hall.

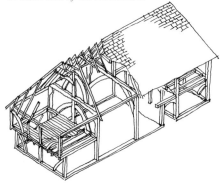

French crown plunged the country into an unjust war, was shrewd commercially. In an attempt to foster English commerce and manufacturing, possibly in the hope of founding a commercial empire which included southern France, the Netherlands and England, he invited the Flemish weavers to settle in England. These settlers brought with them not only their weaving skills but also their considerable buildings skills, the results of which can be seen in Wealden towns and villages such as Cranbrook, Tenterden and Goudhurst. Later in the sixteenth century, the Medicis, the Renaissance bankers of Florence, began to invest heavily in the woollen industry of Europe and much of this money began to flow into England especially Kent. It was a time of stability and prosperity under the strong Tudor rule and this was reflected in demands for better housing generally.

In Kent the yeoman farmer wanted to make his hall house both comfortable and more private. At one end of the hall he inserted another floor. Later on he repeated this at the other end of the hall, leaving the hall open to the roof only in the middle of the house. The storeyed ends of the house were often jettied out over the ground floor, giving the characteristic section to the Kentish yeoman's house. Many have suggested that these jettied wings were created to give extra room, or that the overhang protected the timbers on the ground floor from the rain. It is probably much more likely to have been a technique developed by the carpenter to strengthen the house frame, giving him two places instead of one where joints for the junction of the first-floor sill beam with the wall posts could be made. For his more prosperous client the carpenter carved with elaborate designs the corner posts supporting the ends of the main projecting beams.

By 1600 few houses in the south still had the hall open to the roof. The demands for greater comfort and privacy had changed house plans considerably but the major differences in housing standards still depended largely on the quality of soils and methods of farming. The wealthiest yeomen were to be found in the Weald but the craftsmen and labourers were still comparatively poor. Towards the coast where there was better soil people were less wealthy but the prosperity was more evenly distributed. The houses here were smaller and poorer in quality and more uniform in character than those in the Wealden towns.

The North Downs, Weald and South Downs have always been the richest part of England, not only because of the quality of the soil, but also because of close contact, culturally and commercially, with the Continent. But even the wealthy yeoman farmer of the seventeenth century would improve rather than rebuild his house. The medieval open hall would have a chamber inserted, a hall fireplace and brick chimney would be built, a staircase

Typical Essex house plan of the sixteenth century with a lobby entrance

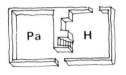

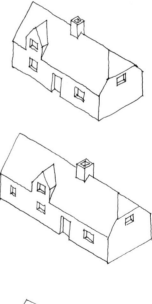

By the seventeenth century the house was built with a buttery off the parlour

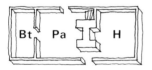

In the seventeenth century this house was enlarged and modernized. It is a typical medieval house improved by the insertion of brick chimney stacks and a chamber over the hall.

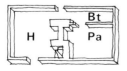

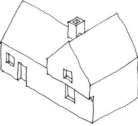

constructed, while dormer windows would be built in the roof to light the new chambers. Another improvement in the mid-seventeenth century was the glazing of windows.

By the early seventeenth century the Kentish cloth industry had passed its peak, but the mixed-farming economy on the richer soils of the coastal belt was thriving. Here the single-storey labourers' houses of Elizabeth I's reign had lofts inserted. These were later replaced by two-storey houses. Any further expansion was usually in an outshut to the rear under a lean-to roof. Like the labourer and husbandman, the craftsman whether rich or poor had a stake in the land, supplementing his craft by farming. The wealthier had separate workshops but most had a workshop in one room of the house.

The tiling of roofs began to replace thatching, but brick building was still rare. While the sixteenth century saw the use of more horizontal timbers and squarer panels, the seventeenth century began to see the framework of the traditional building actually plastered over. The old wattle-and-daub panels had deteriorated and were replaced by an infill of brick nogging which was laid either horizontally or in diagonals, by other decorative patterns, or by plastering. The plaster was laid thick while cow hair, chopped hay or straw was mixed with the plaster to make it strong. In Essex, like Suffolk, pricked, scratched and embossed patterns known as pargeting gave the plaster finish a fine decorative quality. Herringbone scalloped fans and interlacing squares were the favourite patterns. Another unusual method, found at Chiddingstone in Kent, was to form panels in the rough surfaces by pressing flat boards into the plaster, leaving a smooth incision.

During the 1630s the economy of the coastal villages had been more profitable but the improved farming techniques of the yeoman farmer began to enrich the late-seventeenth-century Wealden villages. Houses were planned to include parlours while many timber-frame buildings had their plastered walls weather proofed with tiles or boards.

Tile hanging was rare north of Surrey, Kent, and East and West Sussex, and even here it was a luxury before the seventeenth century. The plain tile is common but decorative patterns were achieved by combining plain tiles with decoratively-shaped tiles. The lightweight timber-framing techniques of southeastern England in the early nineteenth century were particularly suited to tile hanging, seen at its best in places such as Groombridge and Lewes. The mathematical tile was developed for the more fashion-conscious. Like plain tiling, it was nailed to wood lathing, but the tile was shaped in section to give the appearance of brickwork. It was introduced to the southeast in the mid-eighteenth century and was used well into the nineteenth century. It was an inexpensive way to make a timber-frame building more fashionable while avoiding the brick taxes. In towns it was usually confined to the front façade of houses. Tell-tale signs of walling clad with mathematical tiles can be seen in the detailing around windows which usually shows the shallow depth of walling.

In Essex weatherboarding, a covering of overlapping horizontal boards to

Above right. *Decorative tile hanging on a house near Cranbrook, Kent*

Below right. *Weatherboarding on a house at Biddenden, Kent*

throw off rain from the walls, had been used to protect windmills and watermills since the fifteenth century, while from the sixteenth century onwards most farm buildings in Kent, East and West Sussex and Surrey were using weatherboarding. But it was not until the development of lightweight timber-frame construction in the late eighteenth century that it was used for domestic buildings. The finest examples are found in Goudhurst, Tenterden and Cranbrook in Kent. Early weatherboarding pegged to the timber frame was usually made of oak or elm, but later deal, a cheap soft wood, was used nailed to studs.

Further west, in Hertfordshire, Buckinghamshire and Bedfordshire there are some fine timber buildings but the belt of limestone and clay which starts at Portland Bill on the south coast and runs northeastward through the Cotswold country and the high parts of Northamptonshire provided an abundance of magnificent building materials. During the seventeenth century stone was still used mainly for the larger houses. A characteristic of this period was the gabled dormer. The dormer had been invented in the Middle Ages as a device for making more headroom within the roof space and in the limestone regions it was built with a gable of stone flush with the façade of the house. However, in Ashwell, Hertfordshire, there are some late-seventeenth-century cottages with bold rustic pargeting. Many of the poorer houses and cottages in Buckinghamshire were built like the cob houses of Devon but of a white clay known as wichert usually found about eighteen inches below the surface of the ground. By the late eighteenth century and early nineteenth century the first of the cottage rows or semi-detached cottages were built in places such as Ampthill, Elstow and

Weatherboarded cottages, Fyfield, Essex

Part of a group of eight semi-detached cottages built of timber and brick between 1812 and 1816 at Ampthill, Bedfordshire. Each cottage is of one cell and one storey with an attic. Originally the entrance door was in the gable wall.

Great Barford. The two-storey elevations were usually symmetrical, invariably of slight timbers with wattle-and-mud infill, but plastered from the start. By the mid-nineteenth century most of the smaller houses and cottages were built of local bricks.

With the growth in the countryside of such industries as textiles, mining and iron manufacture, the level of employment was affected by booms and slumps in trade. The decline of the obsolete textile, and coal and iron industries of Kent and Sussex gave rise to growing unemployment which resulted in the

*Plan of Whiteley Village, Surrey, built by
William Whiteley in 1907. The design follows
closely the utopian rhetoric of Renaissance
town planning.*

Labourers' Revolt of 1830. Many cottages deteriorated during this period and few new ones were built.

In the more prosperous areas of Buckinghamshire and Bedfordshire, the mid-nineteenth-century landowner, realizing the importance of providing adequate housing for his employees, began to build model villages. The most famous were the Bedford Estate villages – Crawley, Ridgmont, Willington and Woburn. Other landowners built villages such as Leigh (1866) in Kent, and Chenies (1840s), in Buckinghamshire. The railway companies also built a model village at

Woburn Sands in 1846. The tradition was continued in the twentieth century and examples are found at Whiteley (1907), in Surrey; Aylesham, Kent, which was a colliery village built in 1920; Crayford Garden Village, Kent, built for Vickers munition workers in 1914; Shortstown, Bedfordshire, built by the aircraft manufacturers, Short Brothers, in 1917, and in 1927 the village of Stewartby, Bedfordshire, was built for the employees of the London Brick Company.

A peculiarity of the 1920s was the rise of the resort village, an instant village of caravans, stores and pubs, but in

*The neatly composed paths and gardens, and
the elegant Dutch gabling on the almshouses at
Whiteley, are far removed from the traditional
village and cottage. The concept is more a
product of the garden city dream.*

1965 an attempt to build a new model
village was begun by Span, the development company, at New Ash Green in
Kent. But by now the whole notion of
what a village was had been lost. The new
village was no longer the centre of rural
life, but a dormitory town for urban man.

The estate-village concept was continued but by now the new landowner was
the development agency capitalizing on
the sale of houses. The market forces
dictated size, shape and form. With the
new materials anything could be done
and nearly everything was done. The

nineteenth-century philanthropist retained some sort of control but in the
twentieth century no one seems to care
too much. A final attempt to set some
kind of standard was made by Essex
County Council during the early 1970s.
But the plans they produced, harking
back to the picturesqueness of the late
eighteenth century, seem to have chan-
nelled everything into a straitjacket of
mediocrity. This, coupled with the ever-
increasing use of books of standarized
house plans, seems to indicate the rather
gloomy future.

New Ash Green, Kent. The model is more an urban cul-de-sac than the traditional village ensemble, although it was intended to be a village.

East Anglia and the Fens

Marsh and forests dominated the eastern counties until comparatively recent times. When Elizabeth I made one of her elaborate journeys into Suffolk she rode through continuous woodland. Until the Railway Age, centuries of travellers had bypassed the eastern counties. Traders, settlers and invaders usually travelled along a track called the Icknield Way, 'a major route between forest and fen which followed a low chalk ridge sweeping up from the North Downs, crossing southern Cambridgeshire and finally joining the Lincolnshire Wolds. But gradually the character of East Anglia changed as generations of forest-born carpenters building the wooden ships, houses and barns and elaborate engineering masterpieces like the oak structure balancing Ely's lantern, helped turn the oak forests of East Anglia into the wheatlands of today.

Eighteenth-century Norfolk played a large part in the Agricultural Revolution. Corn used to be sown by throwing handfuls of seed on the ploughed land. This was wasteful as much seed was eaten by birds; it was unevenly sown and strips had to be weeded by hand. Jethro Tull (1674–1741) believing that a field would not need to be left fallow one year in three if the soil was ploughed and hoed while the crops were growing, invented a horse-drawn hoe and a seed drill. This meant that the seed was buried and the corn grew in even rows enabling the ground to be hoed in order to kill the weeds. Crop production was doubled with only a third of the seed but this method was little used

until the nineteenth century. The new methods for sowing and cultivating crops required large-scale farming. The open-field system of scattered strip farming gave way to large enclosed farms. As tenancies lapsed small farms were amalgamated into larger units. The peasant farmer became a landless labourer or a worker in the new mines and factories elsewhere.

But East Anglia has always been used to change. Her prosperity during the late Middle Ages was based on the manufacturing revolution created by the Flemish weavers. The peasants here were as rich as those of Kent, but this wealth had yet to contribute to a comfortable standard of living.

Building, especially of cottages, reached its peak between 1580 and 1630. Standing amid the cornlands east of the River Stour are the great wool churches built by the prosperous clothiers who lived and worked in this corner of the country. Their fine wood and plaster houses line the streets of Sudbury, Bildeston, Boxford and Kersey. The richest peasants lived in the thickly-populated villages of the Lincolnshire marshland, the coastal fringe between the Wolds and the sea. During the late sixteenth century they were, like farmers everywhere, profiting from the inflation in prices. But for the poor life was hard. Many kilns and barns were converted into cottages for the poor while others had simple two-roomed houses. They lived in one room and used the second as a work room. An upper chamber was

Previous page. *Chippenham, Cambridgeshire. This was one of the earliest model villages built at the beginning of the eighteenth century. The cottages are mainly one-and-a-half storeys in height.*

added to this basic hall and parlour. The poorer weaver used this upper chamber as a bedroom and he placed his loom below. Few houses had kitchens. The wealthy weaver often had a shop, sometimes separate from the house, where he would probably have two pairs of broad looms and two pairs of narrow looms. For the sailors, fishermen and others who lived by the sea there was a towhouse where ropes (or tows), fishing nets and gear could be kept.

The one-room cottage was common in the Lincolnshire Fens. Cow dung was burned as fuel. A scheme was launched early in the seventeenth century in James I's reign for reopening the Foss Dike, the Roman canal from the Trent to Lincoln, to bring cheap coal in from Nottinghamshire.

The smallholdings of the peasant farmers prospered on the rich soil around the Wash and here the wealth was more evenly distributed. Small farmers made a

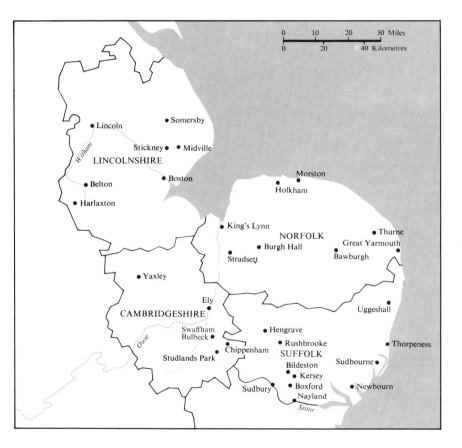

Overleaf. *Houses lining the main street in Kersey, Suffolk*

good living from the land. Their comparative prosperity, which enabled them to resist being swallowed up by the larger farms, accounts for the fact that many small houses continued to be built in this area well into the nineteenth and twentieth centuries. By the early seventeenth century the backhouse, a service room added to the rear of a house, had become a combination of a kitchen, milkhouse and buttery. A second chamber, for storage or sleeping, was added over the hall but many people, particularly in Lincolnshire, were reluctant to sleep upstairs at this time.

Many timber houses built between the fifteenth and seventeenth centuries have infill panels of brick nogging set at angles or in a herringbone pattern between the posts. More often wood lathing is used and plastered flush with the timber posts. As timber became scarce thinner posts were used, the panels widened and the plasterer began to plaster over the timber frame to hide these thinner posts. Incised patterns created by combing the plaster developed into the rich raised-plaster relief work known as pargeting. It was first used in Elizabethan times and was most popular in the seventeenth century but it went out of fashion in the eighteenth century as brick-built houses superseded half-timbering.

In Cambridgeshire, Norfolk and Suf-

A Norfolk reed-thatched cottage at Thurne. Rafters and lath form the base of the thatch which is covered with bunches of reed placed butt down along the eaves and fixed with hazel sways.

folk, many houses were built of clay lumps which were larger than bricks but like bricks they were pressed into moulds. The walling was usually raised two feet above the ground on a flint wall called a pinning. Sometimes a brick plinth, tarred to make it more weatherproof, was used. Not only were the buildings warm in winter and cool in summer but the clay lumps used were comparatively cheap. The floors of most houses were usually earth. When transport became cheaper, limestone was imported from the south Lincolnshire quarries and brick flooring was popular by the late seventeenth century.

The thatched roof is a distinctive feature of Norfolk. Here the reeds are often laid in decorative patterns and hazel spars were used for additional decorative patterns at ridge, eaves and verge.

In the early seventeenth century the large farmer began to dominate the smallholder in the southern parts of East Anglia. Rising prices and the collapse of the Suffolk wool empire added to the growing bitterness among the peasants. It was at this time that the Dutch engineer Vermuyden and the Lord Chief Justice, Sir John Popham, began the process of land reclamation in Norfolk by creating the complex of dikes, cuts and sluices.

The importation of building materials in the late seventeenth century, particularly from Holland, gradually changed the character of local buildings. The traditional materials were chalk, clay and wood. The chalk produced the flint-built cottages and the clay provided the brick surrounds for doors and windows. The combination of the two stood up well to the notorious east winds of Norfolk. Pebbles had been used for building in Norfolk since Saxon times but now brickwork was used to create elaborate chequerboard designs or to give horizon-

Typical nineteenth-century smallholder's cottage built in the Lincolnshire Fens at Stickney

tal lacing courses running through the flint walling. Sometimes stone would be used. In more superior work a tracery of thin limestone was combined with the flint. The clays produced the great variety of coloured bricks used, first in the fifteenth and sixteenth centuries to build the great houses like Oxburgh Hall and Blickling Hall, then, later, to build the small house and cottage, and these local clays were also used for the pantiles which were fashionable in the seventeenth and eighteenth centuries.

Dutch fashions which spread through the area were introduced by the Dutch communities that had settled in East Anglia in towns like Great Yarmouth which formed commercial ties with Dutch, German and Flemish towns. Many Englishmen also made the journey across the North Sea – gentlemen and their servants off to fight in Germany, merchants and their agents going to Rotterdam or Antwerp, shipowners and their crews trading with the Low Countries. The ships brought back Dutch bricks and pantiles to Great Yarmouth, King's Lynn or Boston. The curved gable soon became a characteristic feature. A

Above. *Flint walling on a cottage at Uggeshall, Suffolk*

Left. *Characteristic flint walling with brick surrounds to doors and windows at Morston, Norfolk. Note the pantiles on the roof.*

variation of this was the tumbled gable which, without adding a coping or covering on top of the wall, was the smoothest way to finish a straight gable.

The winds in this part of the country are severe and to prevent the thatch or tile being lifted, gables were nearly always taken up above the level of the roof. This

Brick cottage with pantile roof at Stradsett, Norfolk. Note the parapet wall and 'tumbled in' gable end.

Semi-detached cottages built in Lincolnshire, 1793

A group of cottages at Hengrave, Suffolk

was even more important for the pantiles which were hung on laths and not nailed. Another influence of trade with the Low Countries was the mansard roof. It had been used in England before the middle of the sixteenth century in the Great Hall at Hampton Court, but the examples found in East Anglia were influenced by the Dutch town house. It was an economical design providing a usable space with ample headroom within the roof which avoided the necessity of constructing dormer windows.

By the middle of the eighteenth century the enclosure movement was gathering momentum. In the open village the married labourer would often build his own cottage, while the unmarried labourer would be housed in the parlour or garret of his employer. In some cases dormers were added to the mansard roofs. In the closed villages the building was developed by the landlord himself.

The land was, by now, sufficiently well drained and farmers began to develop ways of revolutionizing the agricultural economy. The Flemish farmers had been intensively cultivating their poor sandy soils since the Middle Ages. Their now flourishing commercial farms gave inspiration to the English farmer. The soils of East Anglia were equally thin and infertile. In 1778 Coke of Holkham began farming on this poor soil. By digging the underlying marl and spreading it over the sandy top-soil he was able to convert it into rich cornland. He adopted the four-year rotation developed by Charles Townshend whereby turnips were cultivated one year, then barley, clover and wheat. Encouraged by the low corn prices, expanding markets and the conversion of some arable land to pasture, the Norfolk four-course, as it was known, was well established by the turn of the nineteenth century.

Early-nineteenth-century cottage of two rooms built at Midville, Lincolnshire

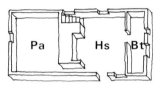

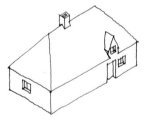

House built of mud and stud at Somersby, Lincolnshire in the early seventeenth century. Externally the studs are concealed by the mud rendering, internally the studs are exposed.

Detail of a cottage roof, Suffolk

But the Norfolk system required more labour and this labour force had to be housed. The agricultural economy was prosperous and the landowner could, therefore, afford to develop more radical solutions to the problems of housing. This resulted in model villages like the estate village of Holkham (1760s) built in a superior Tudor-style of semi-detached and detached cottages lining the entrance to the park gates. But the model village was not new. Some, like Chippenham (1702) in Cambridgeshire, were more a product of emparking when an existing village was swallowed up by the new park and lake, and a new village built nearby. In 1729 Sir Robert Walpole built two rows of cottages, almshouses and two farmhouses at the gates of his mansion, Houghton Hall. The cottages were spacious and outside each a strip of land was provided for cultivation. Housing standards in these new estate villages were superior in comparison to others.

This tradition of estate-built cottages continued throughout the nineteenth century and into the twentieth century. Many villages such as Belton in Lincoln-shire, adopted the Tudor- and Jacobean-style of housing which was fashionable in the early nineteenth century, but later villages were more austere in style. By the turn of the twentieth century the estate village of Thorpeness in Suffolk was built as a resort; Newbourn, Suffolk, was built by the government in the 1930s to help unemployed miners. The village of Rush-brooke, Suffolk, was built by Llewelyn-Davies and Weeks in the 1950s for Lord Rothschild. The buildings are simple and utilitarian, the pitched roofs and white-washed walls follow the same strong traditions of the country craftsmen. But the most ambitious, and most recent, is Studlands Park (near Newmarket), Cambridgeshire. It is a Bovis village development designed by Ralph Erskine, which was begun in 1968. Over nine hundred houses were planned with shops, a pub and village green. The colour-washed walls and brick gabled ends of the cottage are re-used in a fresh and invigorating manner. The style is, however, utilitarian and austere and in marked contrast to the romantic picturesque cottages of late-eighteenth-century pattern books.

The model village of Rushbrooke, Suffolk

Wales

The Normans had already broken up the old monastic structure of the Welsh bishoprics when Llywelyn the Great, in an attempt to create a more stable agricultural settlement, speeded the break up of the old pastoral and tribal world in favour of a more manorial and feudal system by urging the accession of a single heir in preference to the age-old custom of divided accession. Within two centuries of the Norman Conquest this system too began to decline. Those bondsmen who survived the Black Death could no longer be kept in conditions of servitude. The result was a new class of peasant farmer living independently in scattered farms on the lower slopes of the hills away from the old, and now deserted, manorial centres.

Until more permanent building materials were used for cottage building in the fifteenth century the Welsh peasant, like those almost everywhere, lived in a small hut made of tree branches and covered with thatch or turf. They were cheap, easy to build and usually lasted the year out. However, towards the end of the Middle Ages, the hall house was found, primarily in the north and east. It was used by both peasantry and gentry alike. Most were built of cruck constructions. The collar-beam truss raised high on a stone wall replaced cruck framing towards the northwest while along the borderland cruck-framed half-timbered houses were characteristic.

The fireplace was an open central hearth, the smoke escaping by a louvre or vent in the gable. The open hearth fire and

Hall houses, like this one at Llaneilan-yn-Rhos, Clwyd, were the ancestors of the sub-medieval storeyed house.

Early hall house, typical of North and East Wales. The ground floor of each end unit is divided into two small rooms. This kind of hall, with secondary units in line with the main hall, are more numerous than halls flanked by projecting wings of the later Middle Ages. Note the smoke, the open central hearth was vented through a hole in the roof.

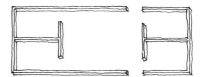

Previous page. *Portmeirion, Gwynedd, designed by Sir Clough Williams-Ellis. It is an amalgamation of seventeenth- to twentieth-century architectural relics relocated in a hillside setting reminiscent of Portofino in Italy.*

the absence of glass produced a simple technology evident in the plan and detail of the hall. Windows and doors were arranged symmetrically opposite each other on the two long walls. The draught was controlled by shutters; windows on the leeward side would remain unshuttered so as to let in light while on the windward side they would be shuttered.

Llywelyn the Great who died in 1240 controlled a virtually independent Wales. Llywelyn II, who was Llywelyn the Great's grandson, profiting from Henry III's troubles with his barons, assumed the title of Prince of Wales. After a series of diplomatic blunders and one unsuccessful revolt, a second rising was attempted in 1282 which was crushed by Edward I, Llywelyn was killed and Welsh independence lost. There was another attempt in 1400. The revolt was led by Owain Glyndwr, the only man of his time capable of creating an independent Wales. The epic struggle that followed lasted for years but by 1410 it was all over and Owain was on the run as

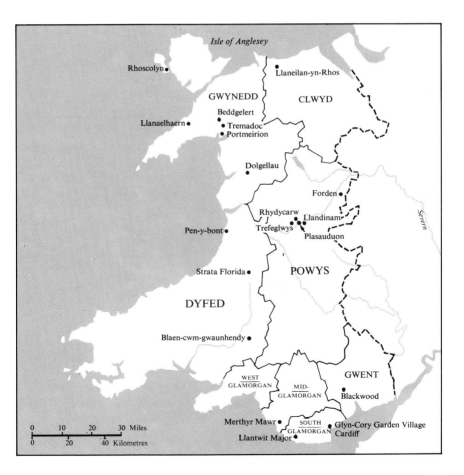

a hunted outlaw. The damage it did crippled Welsh life throughout the fifteenth century. But in 1485 Welsh fortunes turned for the better when Henry Tudor, a descendant of the chief administrator of Llywelyn the Great, defeated Richard III at the Battle of Bosworth Field and took the English throne.

Under the Tudors the Welsh naturally became strong supporters of the crown. When Henry VIII dissolved the monasteries, which in Wales had long since ceased to be a power in the land, he met no opposition. This loyalty to the Tudors was transferred to the Stuarts and despite much criticism of Stuart policy they backed their cause during the Civil War.

At this time quite substantial storeyed houses were found in eastern Wales while the characteristic single-storeyed cottages predominated in the west. The east is a land of timber building while in the west mass construction with earth or stone is typical. In the fifteenth century the storeyed houses along the borderlands of East Wales resembled the black-and-white house of the West Midlands. The timbers were generally large and square. The panels between were filled with wattle daubed with clay. The major differences were in the spacing of the studs, the vertical timbers within a framed partition; close studding, which was more expensive, belonged primarily to the wealthier classes. The wider spacing of studs, which was more economical, made the panels squarer and provided the carpenter with further options for infilling. One distinctive feature was the zig-zag studded infilling. The soil in this part of Wales was richer,

A house with a cross passage behind the central fireplace and chimney. This is a very typical type of plan in Glamorgan.

A cottage at Beddgelert, Gwynedd, dated 1791.

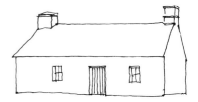

The commonest cottage dominant in the west has a gable fireplace. The entry is also away from the fireplace as in this cottage at Rhoscolyn, Anglesey, in Gwynedd.

A seventeenth-century cottage at Llantwit Major, South Glamorgan.

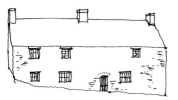

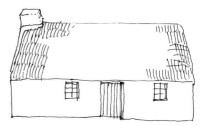

the weather kinder, while the comparative easy access to the rich markets and cities of the West Midlands naturally had a great impact on the buildings of gentry and peasantry alike. The great oak forests of the border areas provided an abundance of material and, of course, the closer contact with the more sophisticated ideas of southern England meant that house plans here were considerably more advanced than those in the west.

In the west the poor soil and weather, the difficulty of communication and the limitation of materials resulted in comparatively poor single-storey buildings until recent times. In Pembrokeshire, in Dyfed, the major advance in the early sixteenth century was the introduction of the fireplace, resulting in the characteristic square or cone-shaped chimney, no doubt modelled on the cylindrical chimneys of the castles and first-floor houses of the aristocracy. These chimneys, often huge, projected outside the end wall of the houses. Fireplaces were often up to eight feet in depth, sometimes incorporating two or three large ovens.

The poor soil and unfavourable climate of the mountainous regions of the northeast attracted few settlers. There was considerable sheep farming here, and during the early Middle Ages much of the wool was exported raw. The abundance of waterpower and the development of the fulling mill were responsible for the rise of the textile industry here. Other types of industry drifted northwest compensating to an otherwise poverty-stricken area.

Although the Welsh fought on the losing side during the Civil War in the seventeenth century their economy soon recovered. Most of the battles of the war were fought outside Wales, there was no scorched-earth policy to match the one following the Glyndwr Revolt and what

wounds there were were soon healed in the predominantly agricultural and pastoral community. There were lead mines in Cardiganshire in Dyfed and small industries scattered here and there in South Wales but, like their forefathers most people lived directly off the land. Free entry to the English market had

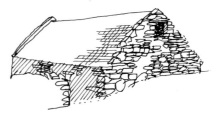

A field house near Dolgellau, Gwynedd

Typical medieval house which must have once been common all over the old county of Pembrokeshire in Dyfed. Note the characteristic round chimney.

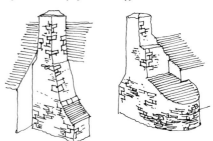

Square chimneys found in Dyfed

137

encouraged the development of a flourishing trade. The sheep on the uplands produced the wool, while the textile industry developed the cloth for export. There was a thriving trade in corn and dairy products but the major industry was provided by the black cattle of Dyfed and the western counties that were driven into England for sale. As London and the Midland cities grew, the cattle became of prime importance to Wales. Vast herds were driven along the mountian tracks across the border with England, the herdsmen bringing back the much-needed cash.

A characteristic of the pastoral economy was the simple circular or rectangular huts, called hafod. Usually no more than ten feet in diameter they resembled the round houses of the Iron Age Celts. Herds and flocks were moved from the valley in the spring to feed in the mountain pastures. The family, or part of it, would take up summer residence in these simple upland dwellings. Furniture was usually made of stones, the fire was situated at one end with a smoke hole in the roof above. The enclosures in the late eighteenth century, the growth of sheep farming to supply the wool for the looms during the Industrial Revolution and the development of more permanent farms ended the summer migrations.

The farmhouses were simple and robust in design. Most had a byre and other farm buildings were planned and built in a single range. Such buildings were confined to the less wealthy farmer working on the poorer land in the uplands. Buildings in the late sixteenth century were still largely medieval in character and the single large room continued to dominate the plan. Gradually the hall was chambered over and the storeyed house became typical for the rural middle classes. But by the seven-

House and byre homestead, Llanaelhaearn, Gwynedd. The farm unit is an addition to the original free-standing house.

Three-unit type of house with byre, Llandinam, Powys. The farm unit, again, is a later addition.

A smaller gentry house of the early Renaissance period at Plasauduon (Carno), Powys. The central chimney and lobby entry is inherited from the sub-medieval house of the region.

teenth century the influence of the Renaissance was seen in a consuming preoccupation with the façade of the house and a rationalization of the functions of the room as well as a

A house at Rhydycarw, Trefeglwys, Powys.
Originally the house had one central chimney
but this was removed in the nineteenth century
to accommodate a central staircase.

reconsideration of its basic proportions.

Improved communications spread the new ideas quickly, while the architect with the grand design in mind, tended to overlook the wisdom of tradition and experience in his detailing with the result that many cottages deteriorated. The high-ceilinged rooms were cold and miserable in the northern winter, but the introduction of glazing freed the window in the wall. No longer did the windows have to line up with those on the opposite wall, they became longer and the rooms lighter.

These buildings were in marked contrast to the peasant houses of Dyfed in Carmarthenshire and Cardiganshire. Walls here were usually of cob or stone construction with rounded corners. They were often framed with scarfed or jointed crucks and then covered with a light thatched roof. The roof was finished in a half hip while the fireplace hood, chimney and partitions were built of clay-daubed wickerwork. The walls of the house were normally colour-washed in red, pink or ochre, while the farm buildings themselves were white.

The big boom in cottage building began in the mid-eighteenth century with the break up of the simple pastoral economy by the Industrial Revolution.

The enclosures drove the poor to carve small homesteads out of the inferior soil of the mountains and moors. It was the growth of industry that saved Wales from catastrophe. The country was virtually isolated; the roads were poor and the landowners had little capital to invest in new industry. The money and expertise to expand quarrying, mining, metal working and textile manufacturing arrived from England. The abundance of new jobs not only absorbed the labour force of Wales but attracted a flock of immigrants from England.

Many of the new cottages were found in scattered semi-rural settlements where

Two-unit cottage, Forden, Powys

Three-unit cottage with entry against a central chimney, at Trefeglwys, Powys

Interior of an old house near Strata Florida, Dyfed, as drawn in 1888. Characteristic features are the wickerwork partition and the scarfed crucks, made by joining a blade to an inclined head of a wall post, and securing it with pegs from the underside of the inclined head.

140

House-and-byre homestead at Blaen-cwm-gwaunhendy (Llanfyndd), Dyfed. A characteristic feature is the colouring of the building; the house and entry are painted red and the byre white.

An early nineteenth-century cottage, Isle of Anglesey

miners and quarrymen could supplement their earnings by small-scale farming. These cottages fall into two distinct groups. The first adopted the traditional storeyed house of the poor. They had high-pitched roofs, suitable for thatch, and small, irregularly-placed windows. Partitions were rudimentary, often made of cloth or wisps of straw. Some were able to afford a dresser or a tiered cupboard which was placed where it would serve as a division so that the parlour could be screened off from the entrance. The second group was built primarily in the Industrial Revolution. Roof pitches were lower as slate replaced thatch, windows were larger and more regularly spaced and partitions were of lath and plaster on studded walls or of matchboard or masonry.

The structure of the house was changing. The cottage along the industrial areas of the northeast adopted the lightweight-timber construction of Kent and Sussex. Walls were made either of weatherboarding or of lath and plaster. Elsewhere cottages were built of mass construction.

Soon the canals, and later, the railways enabled coal to be transported down to the sea as easily as iron. Strings of houses wedged the narrow valleys, the coal tips engulfed the hillsides and slowly the strange industrial landscape of South Wales took shape. In North Wales the slate industry expanded rapidly, vast new streets of terraced housing were hastily built to accommodate an increasing work force. With the rapid growth of industry came the rise of the industrial proletariat and the emergence of the first big labour movements in South Wales in the middle of the nineteenth century.

The rise of the coal industry was accompanied by the collapse of the iron industry and its replacement by steel and related technological developments. The population of South Wales began rapidly to expand. Numerous estate villages had been built in the early nineteenth century. William Madocks went bankrupt trying to establish Tremadoc in Gwynedd as a ferry point and port between the Welsh coast and Ireland, but it was the industrial estates that were the most interesting and novel. Blackwood in Gwent consisted of industrial housing based on the utopian ideas of Robert Owen who built New Lanark. Glyn-Cory Garden Village, Cardiff, was one of the many garden villages built in Wales before World War I. The village aimed at combining the elements of town and country and, by definition, heralded suburbia.

For frivolity and fun, the resort village of Portmeirion, Gwynedd, founded and built by Clough Williams-Ellis in the 1920s is the most notable. It is based on the Italian fishing village of Portofino and is made up of relocated buildings dating from 1610 assembled from both town and country. The obvious distortion in scale and design intentions between such diverse architectural relics is more a forerunner for Disneyland than any serious attempt at village planning. For those who really want to learn, it tells us a great deal about the dangers of picturesque ideals. It was there that Noël Coward wrote his comedy *Blithe Spirit* between one Sunday and the next. And that just about says it all.

Above. *A cottage at Pen-y-bont, Llangorwen, Dyfed. The entrance to the house is alongside the fireplace in the gable end. The roof is covered with slate rather than thatch.*

Below. *Gable-end entry cottage at Merthyr Mawr, Mid-Glamorgan. Twentieth-century modernization has included an outside lavatory.*

The Midlands

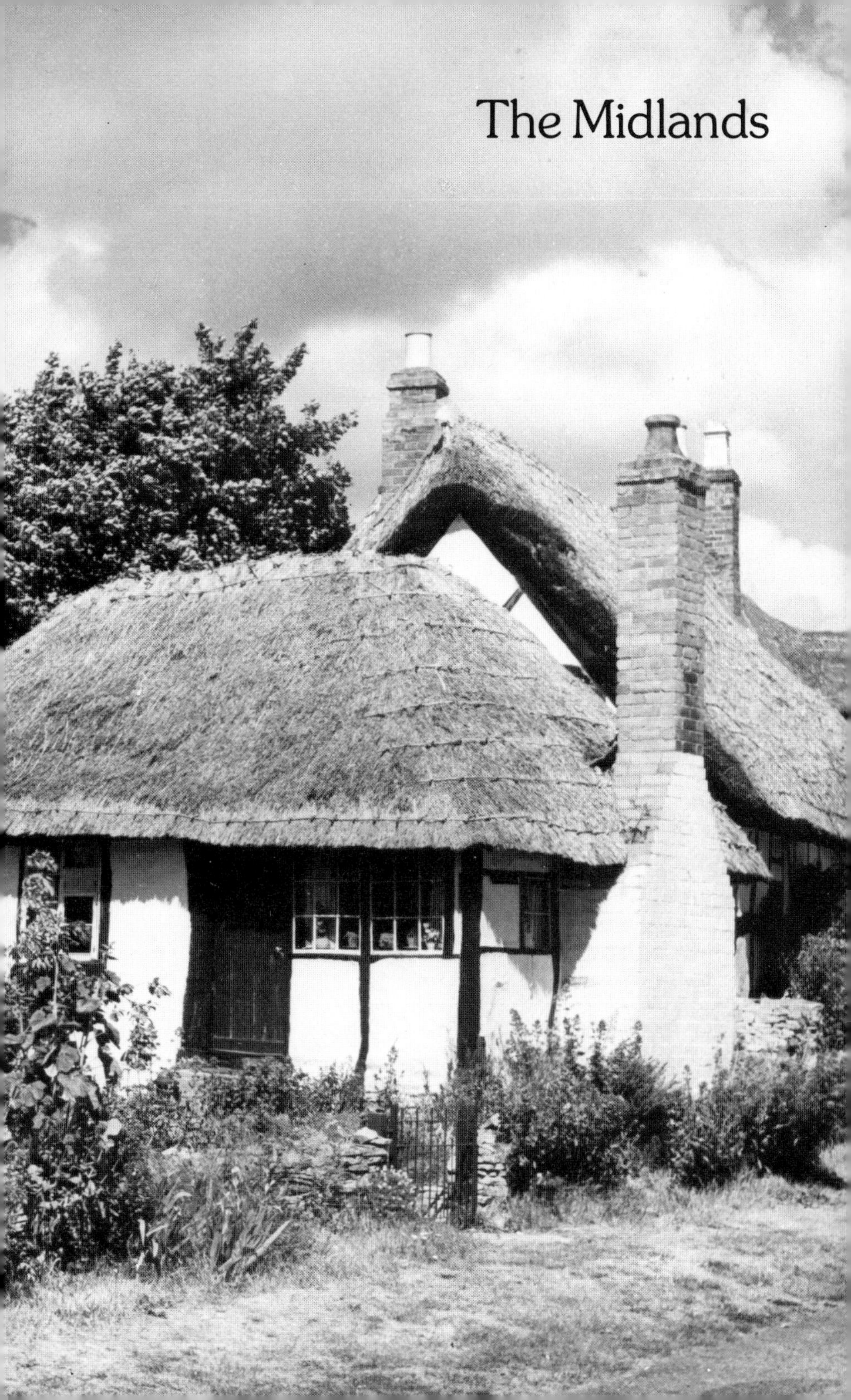

At Laxton, in Nottinghamshire, an example of the old system of land tenure, open-field farming, has been preserved. Under this system three fields would be divided into a number of strips. These were then shared out equally among the villagers, each getting some good and some poor land. Every year in rotation one field would be left fallow while another would be sown with wheat and the third with beans, barley or oats. But the system was very rigid. While the big landowners of Norfolk and the eastern counties were adopting the four-course rotation system in the mid-eighteenth century, the Midlands still retained the open-field system. By the late eighteenth century improved cropping systems were beginning to be adopted, but the slowness to adopt new ideas, the very nature of the soils, the climate, geology, and the comparative late development of the enclosure movement here, had some considerable affect on both the nature

Previous page. *Small thatched cottages at Welford-on-Avon, Warwickshire*

A stone cottage at Sutton Coldfield, Warwickshire. This was built in the mid-sixteenth century as a single-celled cottage of two storeys; there would have been no through passage or partition.

and form of buildings and also the stability of the society itself.

In many districts of England, villages were largely rebuilt during the late sixteenth century and early seventeenth century. But in the Midlands things were in reverse and many villages had declined as a result of the Black Death. This whole process was accelerated by the development of the enclosure movement. Not only did the villagers lose their land but sheep farming, with its comparatively low labour force, created considerable unemployment, forcing many to move to the big towns. Many of the villages today therefore tend to belong to the later and more prosperous period of the late eighteenth and early nineteenth centuries.

By the end of Elizabeth I's reign the single-roomed house of the Midlands had been abandoned in favour of the house with one main room and a parlour. The three-roomed house was common for the more prosperous. Despite the abundance of building stone, in many parts of the Midlands the tradition of timber building was firmly rooted. The stone building of Salop and the brick buildings of Hereford and Worcester were much later. In the fifteenth century the usual form of framing for the houses of the gentry was large framing. Here the framing was left as open as possible, the large panels then being strengthened by angle braces running from the vertical post to the sill or rail below. Small framing was a development of this, the frame being divided into small squares by vertical and horizontal timbers. But the most esteemed form of timber framing in the late Middle Ages was close studding. Here the timber posts were spaced closer together, forming long narrow panels. This was essentially decorative and most of the angle braces were placed internally instead. It originated in the southeast and gradually spread throughout the country. It was, however, expensive and only the wealthy could afford it. In fact in parts of Warwickshire and Salop close studding has been used only on the most important façades.

Large framing was still common in the late medieval house because it was more

Lower Harcourt cottages, Stottesden, Salop, built in the late fifteenth century. Each cottage had an open hall of two bays and a two-storeyed cross-wing. The houses were converted into two during the nineteenth century.

An early-eighteenth-century house, Hereford and Worcester. The walls are in small framing, four panels to the height of the house with long raking braces from the sill to the junction of the walls, plate and posts. Small framing was used as early as the mid-fifteenth century and is typical of the western part of England and in the West Midlands. It was used for large box-framed houses but is more common in small box-framed halls. Buildings using small framing increased throughout the seventeenth century but they were mainly dwellings of one or two cells only.

The White House, Bishop's Frome, Hereford and Worcester, built in the sixteenth century. The panelled framing to the house is an example of close studding with a middle rail. In use before the mid-fifteenth century, it became typical of many buildings built from the sixteenth century onwards, in Hereford and Worcester, Gloucestershire and Salop.

economical. The two most common types were frames with arch-bracing or with tension-bracing; the most typical in the Midlands being the arch-braced frame. In the West Midlands small framing was particularly characteristic of the more important buildings in the late fifteenth century. It was fairly economic and by the seventeenth century the majority of timber-framed buildings in the country were built this way. But these were still quite substantial methods of building houses. Most of the smaller houses and cottages at this time continued to use the cruck-frame method. Some of the best examples are to be found in Hereford and Worcester, often with side walls built at a later date. Along the Midlands and Welsh borders the most characteristic buildings are the black-and-white houses known as

An example of small framing on a cottage at Upton Magna, Salop. Note also the corrugated-iron roof covering which lessens the risk of fire and the cost of insurance today.

'magpie' houses. They are also found across the border in the lowlands and valleys of northeast Wales. The carpenters and builders covered their houses in a beautiful fretwork of black ornamental braces used to support the large timber frames, and they filled the panels between with wattle daubed with clay, and then whitewashed the panels so producing the 'magpie' appearance.

In the larger houses the upper floors were boarded, but in the East Midlands in the late sixteenth century plaster floors which had already been used at Hardwick Hall, Derbyshire, were fashionable. Straw or reed was laid between the floor joists and then covered with two inches of plaster. Rush matting was sometimes laid on the floors.

By the end of the sixteenth century ornamental panelling was common in many of the larger houses. The most typical consisted of a pattern of short curved braces to form circles and lozenges in the square panels formed by the timber frames. Numerous examples are found in Hereford and Worcester, Leicestershire and Salop. A variation was the use of short heavy braces to form star shapes mainly in the northwestern Midlands. In Leicestershire panelling was made decorative with parallel diagonal braces. Many had jettied overhangs, but then these were still fairly substantial houses.

In the southeast timber had already been replaced by brick or stone for the building of the larger houses, but in the Midlands the use of the more expensive forms of timber framing continued to predominate well into the early seventeenth century. But by then the shortage

Woodbine Cottage, Maxstoke, Warwickshire. A cruck-built house probably erected in the early sixteenth century. It originally had a large open hall.

Late sixteenth-century house near Wilmslow, East Cheshire. Note the band of ornamental framing on top of the small framing.

of timber precipitated by the iron-smelting and shipbuilding industries limited the use of timber for building. The result was buildings built with smaller and fewer timbers and squarer panels.

By the turn of the seventeenth century sheep and cattle rearing, and wool and cheese production in the rich pastures of the Trent Valley had made the yeoman of the East Midlands rich. He was both resourceful and ambitious. The open fields were a hindrance and he soon began to enclose them.

Right. *Typical timber-framed cottage in Hereford and Worcester*

The local sandstone northwest of the limestone belt was still fairly expensive material and was used mainly in the larger house. Most cottages were still of cruck construction. In the East Midlands many had lofts or chambers built over the hall and here the cottage was built as a two-storey house. The larger houses had brick chimney stacks built, while current fashion was reflected in the symmetrical arrangement of façades and the addition of storeyed porches. Throughout most of the seventeenth century the majority of buildings in Hereford and Worcester were built of timber but in the southwest many house walls were built of rubble.

By the mid-seventeenth century both the craftsmen and the husbandmen were beginning to suffer from the enclosure of the commons. In Derbyshire the lead mines, in which nearly everyone was involved and without which there would have been no living, had fallen into the hands of richer men. The outbreak of Civil War in 1642, must have come, in some ways, as a relief to many people. Manor houses were fortified while the villages, with the men absent at war, struggled to keep going. After the war the large royalists' estates were broken up. Like the transfer of land following the Norman Conquest and the Reformation the transfer of land during the Commonwealth hastened the growth of larger estates and the inevitable increase of landless labourers.

The more frugal use of timber in building was often concealed behind a façade of plaster or replaced, where possible, by brick. Many village buildings in the stone regions were now built of quarried stone. The farmers on the poorer soils were beginning to concentrate on the more prosperous mutton and wool production, but their increasing wealth was not yet reflected in their

A cottage typical of the Severn Valley. A large chimney stack built out at the gable end is characteristic.

buildings. The timber tradition was still flourishing in Hereford and Worcester, and Salop, but the timber framing was simpler and more uniform in character. The panels were usually about four feet square. A five-storey building would have sufficient height with three panels; often built on a brick or stone plinth, this type of building flourished until the eighteenth century.

Many farmers were involved in fattening cattle brought down from Wales and Scotland for the London market. And of course the growth of industry in Lancashire, Yorkshire, the Black Country, the North Midlands and the northeast coast, provided alternative markets for the farmer. The development by Abraham Darby in 1709 of a method of smelting iron by coke rather than charcoal and the successful experiments with high-pressure steam by Richard Trevithick during the 1790s, resulted in the removal of the iron industry from Sussex to the Black Country in the West Midlands.

The upland areas were given over to sheep to meet the ever-increasing demand of the cloth-producing centres while mutton provided a staple diet for the Durham and Northumberland miners.

Above. *Decorative use of brickwork in an eaves cornice at Barsby, Leicestershire, in 1701*

Below. *Diapering in black headers at Barsby, Leicestershire*

Throughout the North Midlands the land was given over to wheat, barley and oats.

Brick houses, which first appeared in the East Midlands in the early seventeenth century, became more common. Timber-framed buildings were sometimes given a brick façade. Many of the poorer buildings in Northamptonshire were still being built of earth walls, mainly one-and-a-half storeys in height. Some were built of poor crucks. Methods had changed little in this part of the region by the beginning of the nineteenth century.

The major roads in the deep clays of the Midlands and the Home Counties where soft going had long obstructed traffic were now improved by the introduction of turnpikes in the eighteenth century which collected tolls for the maintenance of the roads. The fattening areas of the Midlands were one of the main goals of the cattle drovers. After the Act of Union (1707) Scottish cattle were driven down either side of the Pennines to Lincolnshire, Leicestershire and East Anglia. The Welsh trade goes back to the Middle Ages. The chief route from South and Central Wales for the drovers was through Hereford and Worcester, and the towns of Ross-on-Wye, Ledbury and Tewkesbury to the South Midland grasslands. From North Wales they went through Bromwich and Warwickshire in the direction of Barnet Fair, the Essex grazings and the London butchers. But they kept to the lanes and byways rather than pay tolls on the main roads. Today their routes are marked by the old Drovers' Inns.

While the more advanced and flexible agricultural methods of mid-eighteenth-century Norfolk and the eastern counties were not affected by the low grain prices between 1730 and 1750, the old open-field system of the Midlands too rigid to adapt suffered. Eventually improved cropping

Victorian silkweavers' houses, Leek, Staffordshire. Houses with top shops, where the garrets have been converted, are characteristic of this type of industry.

systems were adopted. Land that could not be tilled was given over to grass for dairying and for fattening the large numbers of lean stock brought into Leicestershire and the Central Midlands from Wales and Scotland. Outbreaks of animal disease, bad winters and periodical harvest failures in the early eighteenth century weeded out many of the small farmers who were subsequently bought out by the larger farms. In the West and Central Midlands, particularly in Leicestershire, Warwickshire and Northamptonshire, the act of enclosure tended to extend the area already under grass and by the mid-eighteenth century there was considerably less farming in the Midlands. The unemployed labourers flocked to the new industrial centres now being opened up by the canals and railways. Large stocking mills were developed at Belper in Derbyshire. Near the mills terraced houses were built for the new workers. But there was a considerable

Eighteenth-century cottage built between house and barn at Exton in Leicestershire

difference between working in their own homes under the dual economy of domestic weaving and working in a factory. Conditions were hard with long hours, poor light and monotonous work.

By the late eighteenth century Wedgwood, Spode, Minton and Copeland, with the ready supply of raw material and new markets, had made great technical advances, and they soon firmly established the pottery industry on the clays of Tunstall, Burslem, Hanley, Stoke, Fenton and Longton. By the end of that century James Brindley's ambitious scheme to provide continuous waterways from coast to coast, the Grand Trunk Canal, was completed.

Stone replaced timber buildings for some of the smaller houses and cottages by the late eighteenth and early nineteenth centuries. In parts of Hereford and Worcester the typical Cotswold detail of the ground-floor bay window combined with the entrance door under the same stone slated hood can be seen. The gabled end of the roof and the sides to many gabled dormers were timber framed with panels of wattle and daub. Windows and doors had elaborate drip-mouldings to protect the head and returns of the opening below. Occasionally a simple projection was provided or, as in Northamptonshire, the stone lintel was more common. Thatch was still a common roofing material, but in the East and Central Midlands it was eventually replaced by the plain tile. In Derbyshire, Northamptonshire and the borderlands with Wales, stone slates are common. Many came from the quarries at Stonesfield in Oxfordshire, or Collyweston in Northamptonshire.

Increasingly manufacturing moved from the domestic system to the factory. In 1762 Matthew Boulton set up his factory by the Birmingham Canal for metal manufacture. The evolution of the invention of the rotary motion by Watt, which was patented in 1781, made possible the age of steam. For the new factory workers, still countrymen at heart, conditions were hard, their freedoms gone. Poor factory conditions and the introduction of new machinery resulted in the Luddite Riots of 1811–12. Rural distress was increased by the enclosures while the high cost of living meant that many were short of food. The new towns were expanding rapidly to cope with the ever-increasing work force for industry. The pressures were great, the misery for many appalling. But the various reform movements and, in the 1870s the first of the model towns, went some way towards appeasing the malcontents. However, the more militant were already active within the labour movement.

The old traditions of cottage building were virtually obliterated through the development of the Hoffmann Kiln (1858) and the rapid use of mass-

Cottages and gardens at Bournville (1879) near Birmingham. Only one survives today.

produced bricks, with the spread of more uniform materials by the canals and railways, and controls imposed by the building bylaws of the 1875 Public Health Act, and with the massive scale of new development. However, a new idea emerged, partly through a twinge of conscience in the Victorian philanthropist and partly through a genuine search for a Utopia. George Cadbury developed at Bournville in Warwickshire the earliest garden village community.

The usual picturesque estate villages had been built in the Midlands, but this was a pioneering development with an emphasis on fresh air, recreation and gardening. It was an attempt to re-create the independence and self-sufficiency enjoyed by the factory worker under the dual economy of the old domestic system. It heralded the later garden city, but it also influenced the later suburban off-shoots and foreshadowed Orwell's totalitarian state, *1984*.

Model cottages for labourers designed at Sudbury, near Derby, in 1869

The Industrial North
and the Moors

The West Riding, an area now covered by parts of North, West and South Yorkshire, has been industrial since the fourteenth century when the iron ore of Sheffield was smelted and made into steel in the homes of the ironmasters. When Edward III invited the Flemish weavers to England, the abundance of both sheep and streams had already made the Yorkshire textile trade a flourishing business. The Flemings taught the English how to spin both finer and greater quantities of yarn from the wool. But the major revolution came in the late eighteenth century and early nineteenth century when a series of inventions made it possible to mechanize the clothing industry. Spinning and weaving were carried out in factories on machines powered first by water wheels and later by steam engines. The West Riding became a vast conurbation as a result of this industrial revolution from handpower to steam.

The monasteries, which had become rich from donations by the Norman gentry, were the great sheep farmers of medieval England. Fountains Abbey, near Ripon in North Yorkshire, owned more than a million acres and over 20,000 sheep. By the sixteenth century the monasteries accounted for one-third of England's wealth. It was because of this wealth together with their obedience to Rome that Henry VIII dissolved the monastic foundations in 1536. But the monasteries had cared for the poor and the needy. After the dissolution crime and vagrancy began to increase and the first of the Poor Laws (1601) was passed authorizing each parish to levy a poor rate and to use it for the provision of

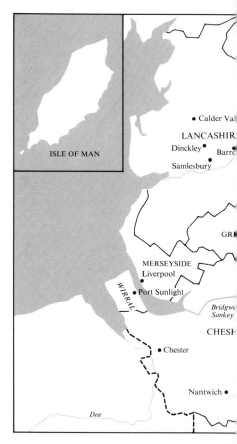

work, relief for the more destitute, the building of houses of correction, and for the apprenticing of pauper children. Numerous monasteries had maintained the roads and many therefore deteriorated following the dissolution. In 1555 the Highways Act transferred responsibility for the roads to the parishes. Few improvements were made and the increased trade which developed in

Previous page. A cottage built of rubble walling and whitewashed typical of the north

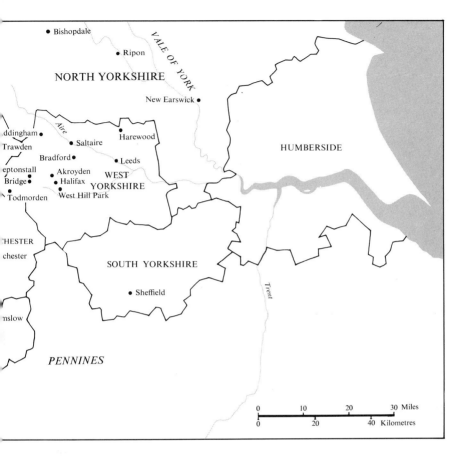

the more settled times following the Restoration (1660) created the necessity for the first Turnpike Act (1663). Under the Act various groups could apply to Parliament for permission to maintain a section of the road and to levy tolls at gates or turnpikes. With the coming of the Railway Age many went bankrupt or were bought out by the railway companies.

While timber-framed houses like Little Moreton Hall in Cheshire (1559–80) were typical mansion houses for the super rich of the period, the farm labourers lived, as they did until the early nineteenth century, in one-roomed, single-storey cottages. The gentry and the rising middle classes were rapidly widening the gap between their living standards and those of the peasantry. In the flat country, timber was the basic building material until the introduction of brick in the sixteenth century. In the hilly counties of the northwest the larger houses of the late sixteenth century abandoned timber for stone. But the poor could afford only the less substantial materials.

The enclosure movement in parts of

161

Lancashire in the seventeenth century was gathering momentum. Many cottages and turf houses were erected on the wastes where the land was very poor. The farmers, scratching a basic living, could only afford a single-storey house. Some had built a chamber over the main room. The traditional peasant's house here and in West Yorkshire was a cruck-framed house between two and four bays in length. Its only distinguishing feature from the barn or hayhouse was the open hearth and it was usually called a firehouse. There was still no division into living, sleeping and service rooms. Many of the smallholders lived in a dwelling known in Yorkshire as a coit. Here the domestic quarters were combined with the barn or shippon under one roof. It was usually built for one of the farm

labourers on the larger farms. The span of the roof was carried on four wooden pillars; the shippon would usually contain stalls for cattle divided from the threshing floor by a heck over which the animals could be fed. House and shippon had their own external doors but in bad weather the labourer would use a connecting door between the two by which to feed the cattle.

The Yorkshire family at the beginning of the seventeenth century still worked and ate in the hall house. Few had a chamber upstairs even for storage, but for the first time the farmer began to separate the byre from the domestic part of the house. A version of this traditional longhouse, a characteristic building in the remoter uplands of Lancashire and Yorkshire, appears in the larger farms of the mid-eighteenth century. It consisted of, for the times, a fairly spacious two-storey house built in one range with a barn. The barn usually had an upper level opening above the barn door for loading hay into the loft.

With the growth of the cloth industry in the mid-seventeenth century and the need for some kind of dual economy to keep above subsistence level, weaving became a common industry in the living rooms of the small farmhouses and cottages as in other parts of the country. But even then many smallholdings failed. The gentry or large farmer began to expand their farms in the upland country of Yorkshire. They had the capital, and now they had the land with which to increase hay production.

A plan of a seventeenth-century house in West Yorkshire. The rear part of the house was built as a continuous range in an outshut. The original plan consisted of a hall, which now included the parlour and the aisle, or corridor. The traditional aisled hall, which was out of fashion by the fourteenth century in the south, was still popular in the Pennine valleys in the seventeenth century. Originally the aisled hall was the house of the nobility in twelfth-century England but gradually it descended through the social scale. Usually it had one or two aisles and was built of stone or timber. In this example the single aisle, originally of timber, has been replaced by a stone wall. The aisle itself becoming a corridor served both the main rooms and the service rooms built under an outshut to the rear.

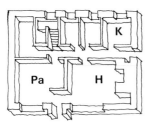

Above right. *Aisled hall at Oakham Castle, Leicestershire. The aisled hall was a characteristic of smaller houses.*

Below right. *Stone-walled aisled hall house at Halifax, West Yorkshire*

In the Bradford area many weavers began to move their looms upstairs. By the late seventeenth century the parlour was added to many house plans. Although it had sitting-room furniture, it was used here as a parlour bedroom, a characteristic of the north. The most common building material for the poor was wattle and daub, but by the early seventeenth century the inclement climate of the moorland and mountain districts necessitated a stronger material and so, where possible, stone was used. In Yorkshire, where an abundance of large blocks was available, walls eighteen inches to two feet thick were invariably built of roughly-squared stones, laid with some attempt at coursing. The stones were left dry outside with rubble, sand or clay as an internal filling. In the Isle of Man many buildings are built of un-quarried stone. Often the walls would be plastered or whitewashed over. The roof would be made of thatch or thick stone plates.

But the stone buildings of the north are

The inside of a sixteenth-century weaver's cottage. Smoke escaped from the fire in a central hearth through the roof.

Left. *Cruck-framed barn with stone walls. It gives a good idea of what the early cruck-framed hall houses must have been like.*

more austere and utilitarian than those in the pure limestone country of the Cotswolds. Most are built of red sandstone or a millstone grit from the Pennines. Chimneys are usually square, often with short, rounded stacks. In Humberside where the only available material was limestone or millstone rubble, sandstone was used for quoins, and for window dressings and doorheads. In the upland areas stone slates replaced thatch for roofing while in the flatter districts of Yorkshire and Humberside, particularly the eastern edge of the Vale of York, pantiles were used as a replacement for thatch in the nineteenth century.

Before the reorganization and subsequent concentration of industry in the towns, the domestic systems in the clothing industry carried out by workmen and their families at home predominated. The merchants collected the wool, took it to the spinners and later collected the yarn they had spun. This was then taken to the weaver's cottage to be turned into cloth. Most weaver's houses, both in the town and country, consisted of a workroom for the looms either in a first-floor room or loft space. The looms were lit by a long row of windows, while some of the lights opened to ventilate the workroom. Sometimes there was a separate access by

A late-seventeenth-century farmhouse built at Samlesbury, Lancashire. It is a small house built of stone. There is no parlour in this example. The entrance at the end of one side is typical of many houses built in the north at this time. A new and widespread feature is the closet to the side of the fireplace on the first floor.

Ground floor

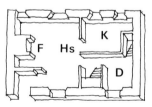

First floor

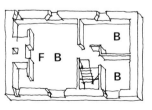

A mid-seventeenth-century house built of random rubble at Bishopdale, North Yorkshire.

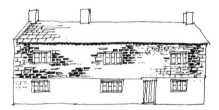

Fisherman's cottage on the Isle of Man. The walls, built of rough boulders found on top of the surrounding ground, are plastered over. Notice the way the thatch on the roof is lashed with ropes, their ends pegged to the walls of the house. The far end section of the house, built with a slate roof, is a later addition.

an external staircase. The more well-to-do weaver often had a separate workshop attached to a conventional house.

But many of the smallholders supplementing their living by weaving were hard hit by the Industrial Revolution. As weaving increasingly moved from the domestic to the factory system so the small freeholders, tenant farmers and commoners were taken over by the large corn-growing and meat-producing farms. The expanding industries needed workers and the workers needed feeding, and this market could only be met by the bigger and progressive farms.

The Weaver Navigation Scheme, and the construction of the Bridgewater and Sankey canals, liberated the north for industrial expansion. In 1764 Hargreaves invented a machine, the spinning jenny, for spinning eight threads at once. In 1769 Arkwright invented the water frame. Crompton then improved on the two by

inventing the spinning mule which revolutionized the textile industry. For the first time both spinning and weaving could be done in factories. Machines were installed, powered first by water and later by steam.

In the early nineteenth century countrymen flocked to the industrial towns for work. Housing accommodation was both poor and scarce. Many lived in cellars or garrets. Conditions were insanitary; water was fetched from pumps or standpipes and terraced houses, including the notorious back-to-back dwellings, were jammed together close to the factory. The back-to-back houses consisted of the simple domestic plan joined at the rear by a duplicate plan. There was no through ventilation as the only windows were on the entrance side of each house. Accommodation consisted of one room up and one room down. Often there was a cellar. There was no

Housing typical of some of the industrialized narrow valleys of West Yorkshire. In this example one row of two-storey houses is built on top of another. Entry to the house on top is from a road at the third-storey level to the rear of the building. These houses were built at Todmorden in 1861.

The notorious back-to-back housing continued well into the present century in some northern towns. In this example in Leeds there is a cellar, a living room and a scullery plus two bedrooms.

167

Terraced housing in old Leeds

sanitation, families sharing a common privy and pump with some twenty other households. Sheffield was one of the first towns to prohibit the building of back-to-back housing in 1864. Many towns began to improve the standard of housing. The typical two-storey worker's cottage had a kitchen combined with the living room, and scullery combined with a wash room. There were two bedrooms upstairs and outside there was an earth closet and coal store. But as industry developed and expanded so the necessary communal services proved inadequate and the conditions generally became insanitary.

Many Committees of Inquiry were set up to study conditions within the industrial towns. The terraces were congested, the dwellings themselves overcrowded. The back alley or street was used for sanitation, but the development of the first of the waterborne-sewage systems virtually eliminated this by making it possible to build a water closet within the house. House plans were rationalized. The two-storey cottage was doubled in size and this basic plan was copied throughout the industrial north.

The Peterloo Massacre, a conflict between the military and the people assembled at a Parliamentary Reform meeting held on 16 August 1819 at St Peter's Field, Manchester

The Hoffmann Kiln made possible a uniform brick which was cheap and mass produced. This new material, transported by the expanding railways to every corner of the country, coupled with the controls imposed by the Public Health Act of 1875, soon took over the remaining strongholds of the traditional methods of building. The towns soon looked very similar to each other and working-class cottages in Leeds were, by now, little different to those of London. The engineering tradition and style of the industrial north had come to stay.

There had, of course, been considerable labour unrest. Adverse economic conditions following the Napoleonic Wars in the early 1800s, the break up of the smallholdings and domestic systems, the misery of working conditions in the new factories, insanitary housing within the new towns, and fear of unemployment with the development of a more mechanized industry resulted in the Luddite Riots of 1811–12, the peaceful hunger march of the unemployed in 1817, the Peterloo Massacre of 1819, and the demands for political reform. The Reform Bill was passed in 1832 but Peel did not repeal the Corn Laws until 1846. Many of the more liberal industrialists, realizing the source of their wealth was in the labour they employed, began at last to provide decent housing to accommodate the workers. Mill villages were built in Lancashire, at Barrow Bridge (1830) and

Calder Vale (1835). There was a model village at Akroyden, Halifax (1859), and a model estate for Crossleys, the carpet manufacturers, at West Hill Park, Halifax in West Yorkshire. Rowntrees' model factory village, possibly the most successful of all was in North Yorkshire at New Earswick (*c.* 1901), designed by Parker and Unwin. But the first industrial village was Saltaire in West Yorkshire. It was built from 1850 onwards by Sir Titus Salt in a valley outside Bradford on the banks of the River Aire. The idealistic expression of Renaissance-palace plans were chosen for both mills and housing. The purity of such classicism was considered by Sir Titus to be the embodiment of his idealism. Here, each house had a parlour, a kitchen and a pantry, three bedrooms and a lavatory outside. The houses were built in terraces and made of stone. Others, like Colonel Edward Akroyd, the textile manufacturer, deliberately mixed the grades of housing so that the wisdom of the better educated and better paid might infect their less-wise neighbours of an inferior social standing. The regional building style had already been engineered and now the society itself was being engineered. But perhaps such an ordered, systematic approach was the only way to contain the highly inflammable economic, political and social pressures of the nineteenth century. Perhaps there were profits to be had in containing it too.

Northumberland and the Lakes

Any improvement in housing standards took time to reach outlying parts of Britain. The cottages of turf or dry-stone walling common in Northumberland and North and West Yorkshire in the nineteenth century were no improvement on the Cornish husbandman's earth-walled, thatch-roofed house of the early sixteenth century. In fact, at the turn of this century bark peelers in Cumbria built themselves temporary huts consisting of one room about thirteen feet long and eight feet wide. The hut was built of four poles lashed together in pairs to support a ridge piece. The walls, two feet high were made of two skins of wattle filled with earth. There was a sod roof. This rudimentary shelter differed little from the poor medieval cottage. The primitive nature of much building in this area in the not-too-distant past is explained by the poor soil in the generally mountainous landscape and its geographical position along the often troubled border areas with Scotland. From Roman times onwards, Northumberland was the frontier land of England's northern boundary, defended first by the legionaries of the Roman wall and later by castles and fortified houses. Raiding, pillaging and murder ravaged the border country during the fourteenth to seventeenth centuries. The Act of Union between England and Scotland in 1707 was intended to end such strife, but small border raiding parties persisted. The powerful families retired inside great castles and the lesser gentry fortified themselves in peel towers or bastle houses where the humbler folk took refuge, if they could, while their huts were being burned and their cattle or horses carried off. It was impossible to develop agricul-

ture under such conditions and it was not until some kind of stability was maintained in the eighteenth century that Northumberland's agriculture was developed. Other areas were much further advanced. In the county of Durham, which had always been a protected part of the frontier, land was enclosed and agriculture developed, villages and small market towns began to flourish.

Most houses during the border troubles were either built impregnable, or made of such insubstantial materials that, when destroyed, they could easily be rebuilt. The earliest defensive settlements here consisted of the barmkin, a sort of timber corral, protected by the menfolk, in which castle and family were sheltered. Timber towers, rather like the medieval castle motte, were built. By the fourteenth century these developed into the fairly substantial peel tower. These towers were built of stone walls, three feet or more in thickness. There was usually a store room on the ground floor, a first-floor hall with a fireplace and some windows, with a bower on the second floor. The occupants bolted themselves inside the towers and relied on the impregnability of the structure itself for defence in times of strife. The ground-floor ceiling was usually stone vaulted so that if the ground floor was lost the upper floors were still protected. Roofs were either pitched and covered with slates or shingles, or flat and covered with lead. They appeared mainly in the fourteenth century when the King began to permit private fortifications near the Scottish border. In Northumberland the peel tower stands on its own as a self-contained residence. In Cumbria, some distance away from the more

Previous page. *A typical cottage in County Durham*

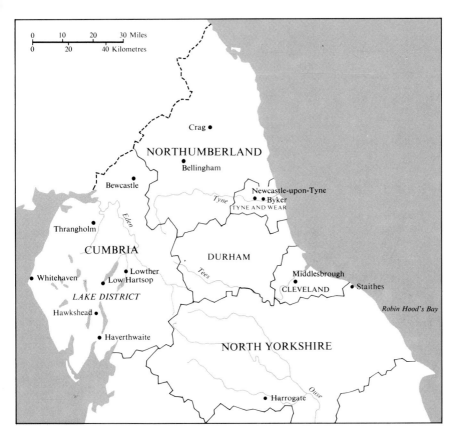

dangerous border area, the tower was often built as an addition to the traditional ground-floor hall house.

A variation was the sixteenth-century bastle house, a defensible farmhouse in which animals were housed on the ground floor, while the first floor contained all the domestic quarters. They are found chiefly in Cumbria and Northumberland and are usually rectangular in plan, about 35 feet by 25 feet, two storeys in height, with steeply-pitched gables. Walls, about four feet thick at the bottom and tapering to three-and-a-half feet at the first floor, were built of large irregular-shaped blocks of stone. Entry to the upper floor was by a retrievable ladder but later an external stone staircase was built. Many had a fireplace, but windows were small. Roofs were of collar and ridge beam, the covering originally of thatch or heather but later replaced by slate.

By the middle of the sixteenth century the larger houses built in the more peaceful parts away from the border area made little provision for defence, although they were still primarily medieval in appearance. By the end of the seventeenth century some began to display

*Detail of stone surround to a doorway in a
bastle house at Bewcastle, Cumbria*

Left. *A bastle house at Bellingham,
Northumberland*

175

*Vaulted interior of a bastle house at Crag, an
isolated upland farm, near Hepple in
Northumberland. The walls are of coursed
rubble.*

details of Renaissance influence. The
typical plan consisted of a parlour, hall
and service room on the ground floor
with bedrooms above. Details and plan
arrangements changed in subtle ways and
by the beginning of the eighteenth
century the large house began to follow
the pattern set elsewhere in England.

One of the characteristics of the areas
of Northumberland and Cumbria close
to the Scottish border in the late sixteenth

century was the seasonal migration of
pastoral people with their herds from a
winter settlement to summer pasture.
During the Middle Ages it was a widespread practice over most of northern
England, but by the sixteenth and
seventeenth centuries it survived in only a
few places. The herdsmen built themselves rudimentary shelters on the summer pastures. These shelters, called
shielings, were built of dry-stone walls,

although some may have been built of turf. The walls were two feet or more in thickness with a long rectangular plan varying from 10 feet by 20 feet to 16 feet by 32 feet. Most corners were rounded. The entrance door was usually positioned down the long wall. Windows were rare. Most roofs were made of thin poles and spars, gabled and covered with turf. An open hearth was planned along one of the main walls. In some shielings a byre was included. But by the eighteenth century a more efficient system of pasture management was developed, and more permanent crofts, similar to those in the Scottish islands, were established.

Travellers who saw the Cumbrian cottages and farms in 1698 say they consisted of one room, built of dry-stone walls. There was no plaster and little, if any, chimney. During the sixteenth and seventeenth centuries cruck construction was common for most of the smaller houses. The walls were either clay and cobble, wattle and daub, turf, or field stones. Based on the hall house, the early plans consisted of one main room with an open hearth or fireplace built on the gable end. Off the main room was a tower with a loft space above. In the agricultural areas of the Lake District a cross passage and byre was added to form the typical longhouse.

Many houses were rebuilt of more permanent materials in the seventeenth century. Cavity walls were built of an outer and inner leaf of rubble and the cavity filled with earth, although stones were used, like the ties to modern brick cavity walls, to bond the two together. The walls of many farmhouses were finished with a thick coat of rough cast lime. The white finish, in contrast to the dark stone of surrounding farm buildings, was a characteristic sight. It became necessary to include an upper storey so

the roof space was lofted over. This space was reached by either a ladder, a stone spiral staircase or by a staircase built out in a projection at the rear of the living room like those in the farmhouses of Guernsey and Jersey. There was usually a large hearth with a timber-framed hood, lined in wattle daubed with clay and mud. Later both chimney and stack were built of stone. The hearth was large enough to draw up chairs beside the turf fire. Often there was a fire window to light the area of the hearth.

Most entrance doors were at the gable end, but gradually the door was repositioned symmetrically in the main façade. A kitchen was added later in an outshut at the rear under a lean-to roof. What decoration there was consisted of a partition of moulded posts and panels between the house and parlour. Sometimes a cupboard was built into it. In a few cases box beds were built into the parlour so that during the day, in order to create more space, the bed could be concealed as if in a cupboard.

The Lakeland farmhouses were the homes of largely independent owner-occupiers, the so-called 'statesmen'. The manorial customs of the Lake District, which permitted the handing down of the farms through the family, meant that many were carefully rebuilt or extended, but by the eighteenth century inflation, mortgage debts and a variety of other problems resulted in many farms changing hands.

Other service rooms were added, either by altering the existing byre or by extending the main house. Roof pitches were altered to give headroom in the loft space for bedrooms. By the eighteenth century storm porches made to keep out the winds were built onto many longhouses. A new entrance was cut and a through passage created. Some farms had

The plans below are characteristic of statesmen's houses in Cumbria. The statesman, the typical farmer of the Lake District, was the customary tenant who had obtained the right to bequeath his land by will and paid only a small money rent in the Elizabethan period. Within a century this new status and security was reflected in his increasing prosperity. The statesmen's houses were now no longer made of mud, but of rubble walls with an earth core.

The farmhouse, rendered with a thick coat of rough cast and limewashed, was flanked by farm buildings. These basic elements were unchanged up to the eighteenth century. An upper storey was necessary, reached usually by a staircase starting in an outshut at the rear or by ladder within the main structure. There are two basic types: a house comprising two main rooms, or a house consisting of three rooms and a cross passage.

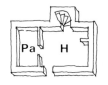

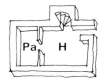

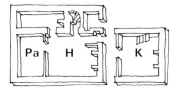

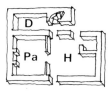

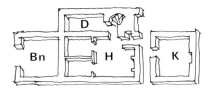

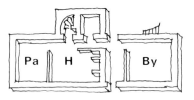

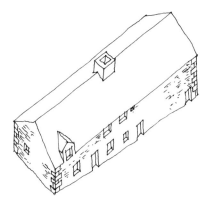

Plans and view of Town End Farm, Broughton-in-Furness, Cumbria

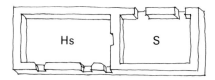

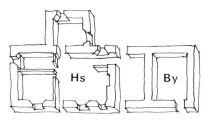

First Floor

Ground floor

a separate barn or byre built some distance away but at right angles to the main building.

By the beginning of the eighteenth century cruck construction was little used except in the clay area of the Solway plain where it was used until the nineteenth century. The walls were two feet thick, built of clay bound with chopped straw; the wall itself being built up in layers like the cob walls of Devon. Nearer the coast a characteristic feature was the rounded cobbles set in clay. Many windows and doors in all but the poorest clay houses were, like the more substantial stone-built houses, dressed in sandstone. In the eighteenth century thatch as a roof covering was replaced by large sandstone flags laid to random sizes. In the cliff villages such as Staithes, and around Robin Hood's Bay off the North Yorkshire coast, roofs covered in pantiles predominate.

Most buildings in the eighteenth century were small, even for the yeoman farmer. It was a poor region; few farmers used labour outside the family and so fewer cottages are found. Most cottages were single storey with only two rooms. The typical plan consisted of a kitchen-living room, a fireplace on the gable wall and a small parlour-bedroom. The entrance door was positioned centrally at the front with a window either side to light the living room and the parlour. By the mid-eighteenth century a two-storey cottage, based on a similar ground-floor plan, was common. A narrow staircase or companion-way ladder concealed in a cupboard led to the upper-floor bedrooms. The single-fronted house, with one up and one down, was a smaller version of this. Many of these were developed in short rows or terraces.

Gradually roads were made, the moorland farms drained, woods planted and

A simple three-unit plan of the late seventeenth century. Improvements were made by the insertion of a bay window in the parlour and the addition of a service wing with a dairy, scullery and cellar.

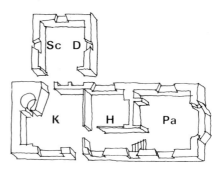

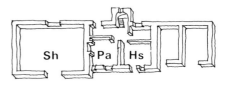

Plan of farm range at Brow Edge, Haverthwaite, Cumbria

View of farm range at Brow Edge, Haverthwaite, Cumbria. The central house is finished in rough cast and limewashed in contrast to the dry-stone walling of the range of farm building built on either side of the house. Typical of farm buildings from the eighteenth century onwards.

the wastelands enclosed. In the late eighteenth century half of Northumberland was still wasteland but by the nineteenth century much of this wasteland had been transformed by extensive cultivation.

Many of the lands confiscated from supporters of the Stuart cause passed into the hands of the newcomers. These newcomers were people who had made their fortunes in the coal and shipping trades of Tyneside and the developing industries associated with them. The new ideas and opportunities were beginning to shape the people, their land and their buildings. Weaving which had been carried on in many farmhouses transferred first to the weavers' cottages and then, with the development first of waterpower and later of steampower, to the factories of the developing industrial centres. An unusual feature of the time is the spinning gallery. It was an open balcony at first-floor level, built of wood. Access was usually from the outside and most faced north and were used for hanging yarn to dry or for spinning.

The outshut, the traditional method for extending the ground floor, was considered wasteful. A two-storey house was developed with four rooms on the ground floor and four above, all contained under one roof. This house type, divided by the entrance and staircase, was used throughout the nineteenth century. The construction in loadbearing brickwork or masonry was virtually universal. Coal replaced peat as fireplaces multiplied and flues were built. Roofs were

covered chiefly in slate while the house plan, which by now was based on earlier traditional plan types, began to be expressed externally in the house façades. As the Durham and Northumberland coalfields expanded, so the pit villages were extended and house types and building materials were mass produced, and by the middle of the nineteenth century the last traces of traditional styles were drained from the terraces of the new industrial estates. The necessity of living near the works meant renting cheap houses in unattractive rows. For the workman the appearance of his

The great problem of finding sufficient housing for the labour force required in the Industrial North was solved by radical rethinking of house design. One result was the back-to-back houses seen at Leeds. Here, in Newcastle-upon-Tyne, we have another variant, the terraced flat. A characteristic feature is the paired doorways. One door leads to the ground-floor flat, the second to the first-floor flat.

Above right. *A house near Harrogate, North Yorkshire, showing an outshut built at the rear*

Below right. *Middlesbrough, Cleveland, one of the industrial centres of the Industrial Revolution*

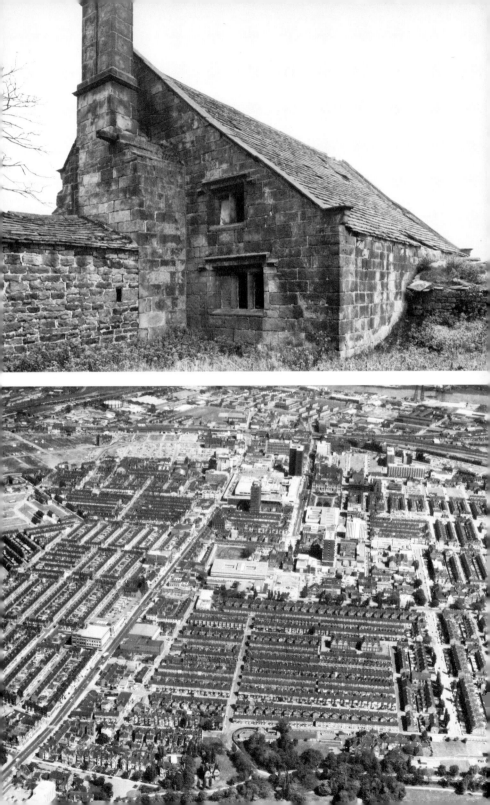

*Lowther Village, Cumbria, built by Sir James
Lowther in the eighteenth century*

surroundings was almost irrelevant, the one absolute necessity was to be at work: otherwise his family would starve. Middlesbrough in Cleveland is a typical industrial centre developed during the Industrial Revolution.

There were numerous model villages built but perhaps the most interesting was the village of Lowther, Cumbria, begun in the 1760s. Sir James Lowther commissioned the Adam Brothers to design the village. They did not make the mistake, like other planners and architects, of using some kind of cosmetic disguise of Tudor or Gothic or of attempting to re-create an idyllic picturesqueness fashionable a little later. Their mistake was in taking the grand design ideas, the circus, the crescent and the square associated with Bath, the epitome of eighteenth-century urbanism, and fashioning the slightly mean labourers' cottages around such notions. Accommodation was reasonable, and private and communal gardens were provided, but the irony in juxtaposing two totally different scales did not appeal to the country people of Cumbria. Clough Williams-Ellis also juxtaposed dissimilar scales at Portmeirion in Wales, in the 1920s. Colour-washed country cottages stand next to relocated classical town houses. This unexpected context turns the whole thing into an entertaining joke at Portmeirion but at Lowther the irony was too strong and the result was desertion and desolation.

Elsewhere intentions were never quite so polemical, but the feelings of feudalism were strong and here, more than anywhere, the tidy groups of estate cottages at or near the park gates seem to reflect the rapport established between landlord and tenant rather than the more obvious divisions seen in the wealthier parts of southern England.

Most new estates today are typical almost of anywhere. The use of pitched roofs and brick and the deliberate wilfulness in plan predominate. The new housing development at Byker in Newcastle, designed by Ralph Erskine, in 1975 is the nearest an architect has come to regaining some of the traditional verve and spontaneity, but the forms taken as a reference are those of the expanding towns of the Industrial Revolution and not the picturesqueness of the rural villages. Perhaps it is not possible or desirable to re-create such an aura.

The Scottish Lowlands
and the Border Country

In the late eighteenth century many of the poorer households still lived in cruck-framed turf houses. In parts of Stirlingshire, now in Central Region, many such houses were constructed not by building up walls of cut turf or peat, but by carving away the surrounding ground leaving only the solid walls of the house. Most turf walls were built up on a foundation of rubble. Some examples survived until about 1860 on Redding Muir and at March End, Polmont in Central Region and another example was found as recently as 1920 at Torbrex, near St Ninians in the same region.

Other materials most readily available were clay and stone. Both were used in the construction of loadbearing and non-loadbearing walls. In Stirlingshire the slightly better-off were able to afford buildings built of clay, tempered with chopped straw as a foundation for rough stone. The walls were non-loadbearing, the roof loads being distributed by cruck trusses to the stone footings. But by the late eighteenth and early nineteenth centuries many of these houses were gradually replaced by dwellings built of more substantial materials. In Ruthwell, in Dumfries and Galloway in southwest

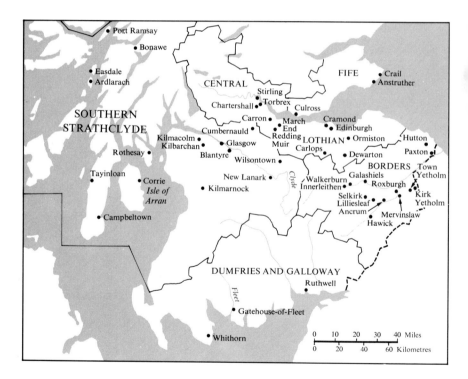

Previous page. *Houses in Culross, Fife. The corbel steps and harled walls are characteristic.*

Scotland, all the houses were built originally in clay, but the *Old Statistical Account* of 1792 describes how many clay houses were rebuilt with stone and slated, and the streets of the village widened and laid in a straight line. Yet at Hutton in Borders Region and Corrie in Strathclyde people were still living in clay-built houses by the mid-nineteenth century. The clay walling in Scotland was a less painstaking and lengthy task than the cob walling in Devon. In Devon it would take several months to build a cob-walled house but in Dumfries and Galloway, as in Cumbria across the border, walls tended to be built in a day as a communal venture, possibly for a newly-married couple or for elderly people. The late-eighteenth-century account from the Dumfries parish of Dornock is interesting:

> The farmhouses in general, and all the cottages, are built of mud or clay; yet these houses, when plastered and properly finished within are exceedingly warm and comfortable. The manner of erecting them is singular. In the first place, they dig out the foundation of the house, and lay a row or two of stones, then they procure from a pit contiguous, as much clay or brick earth as is sufficient to form the walls and having provided a quantity of straw, or other litter to mix with the clay, upon a day appointed, the whole neighbourhood, male and female, to the number of twenty or thirty, assemble, each with a dung fork, a spade, or some such instrument. Some fall to the working of the clay or mud, by mixing it with straw; others carry the materials; and four or six of the most experienced hands, build and take care of the walls. In this manner the walls of the house are finished in a few hours, after which, they retire to a good dinner and plenty of drink which is provided for them, where they have music and a dance, with which, and other marks of festivity, they conclude the evening. This is called a 'daubing' and in this manner they made a frolic of what would otherwise be a very dirty and disagreeable job.

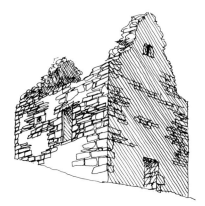

A sixteenth-century peel house, Mervinslaw, Roxburgh, Borders Region

The walls were built in courses on a stone foundation or footing which acted as a damp-proof course. In parts of Berwickshire in Borders Region small stones were mixed with the clay to form a very hard durable material. Despite the quickness of the building process timber shutting was rarely used in southwest Scotland, but in the southeast a system known as cat and clay was common. Here the walls were constructed of bunches of straw mixed with soft clay and packed into a wooden framework of upright and cross spars. Throughout the first half of the nineteenth century most canopy chimneys and internal partitions were built this way. Many of these clay houses, particularly in Berwickshire, were roofed in pantiles, but a covering of straw-and-clay thatch laid over sods was common in Fife and the Kyle and Carrick District of Strathclyde. A characteristic of the Kilmarnock area in this region in the late eighteenth century was a method of thatching with straw and mortar. Thatching was carried out in the usual manner, a mortar mixed with cut straw was then thinly spread over the thatch with a large trowel. Clay thatching was thought a considerable improvement over the more common roped thatch. The floors of the houses were often made of clay, sometimes with a decorative strip of whitening round the edges.

In the eighteenth century fireplaces were still in an open hearth in the centre of the kitchen floor. A wide canopied chimney made of wattle and daub was hung over the fire. By the turn of the nineteenth century the central hearth was being replaced by chimneys built either as a projecting canopy or as an enclosed stone-built flue built on the end walls of the houses.

In the rural areas the longhouse tradition of byre, stable and living quarters under one roof was typical of most farmhouses. The solid cross wall separating the byre from the living quarters was rare but a light partition of wattle and daub was typical. In the old county of Ayrshire, now in Strathclyde Region, it was still customary in the early nineteenth century for the cattle and family to enter the house by the same entrance. Later the byre was built separately and the old byre converted into an additional living room. The solid cross wall became typical, often with a fireplace and chimney built in. The entrance door was usually in the centre of the long wall.

Living conditions for labourers in Roxburgh, in Borders Region, in the mid-eighteenth century were deplorable. Most houses were built of cat and clay. The walls were usually no more than approximately five feet high. Windows were small and few. Most houses were thatched. In Selkirk the Minister of Galashiels wrote in 1797:

Farmhouses in general paultry and ill built. Most of the dwelling houses are of one storey, low in the roof, badly lighted and covered with thatch. The walls, however, are of stone and lime; and of late a few of these low houses have been slated . . . the cottages . . . are wretched habitations, dark, smoky and insufficient defences against wind and rain.

Dalriadic type of black house found in Strathclyde Region, and on the islands of Islay and Jura. They are very similar to some developments of cottage building in the Isle of Man and Ireland. Unlike the black houses of Skye and the Hebrides, the Dalriadic type has gable ends, but is similar to the Skye type in that the thatch is carried over the walls, front and back to form overhanging eaves. Of all the three types of black houses, the gable wall house was the easiest on which to build a fireplace and chimney and thus became a prototype for much cottage building throughout the Highlands. This was later developed by the crofter in the Highlands into a house having an upper storey provided with dormer windows.

Eighteenth-century house at Kirk Yetholm, Roxburgh, Borders Region

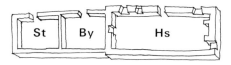

Right. *Long Row, Campbeltown, Argyll. The design is more consciously architectural with strict symmetry. This three-storeyed block was built in the early nineteenth century. The walls are harled with partly exposed coursed rubble.*

*Campbeltown, Argyll, Strathclyde Region, in
1867. Many settlements were laid out along
fairly ambitious lines. The planning was more
akin to eighteenth-century urban design than
the traditional village plan.*

In Stirlingshire many of the farm tenants had to provide their own accommodation. The Reverend Patrick Graham writing in the late eighteenth century, described some of these:

... the houses of the peasantry were wretched huts, thatched with fern or straw, having two apartments, only, the one a kitchen ... the other a sort of room ... where strangers were occasionally received, and where the heads of the family generally slept. The byre and stable were generally under the same roof, and separated from the kitchen by a partition of osiers wrought upon slender wooden posts, and plastered with clay. A glass window and a chimney were esteemed a luxury, and were seldom met with.

In many parts of Argyll herdsmen continued to build sheilings until sheep farming was replaced by cattle farming during the late eighteenth century. The deserted shieling huts are numerous and widespread in the pastures of the uplands.

Development in the urban centres was vastly different to that in the rural areas. More substantial materials were being used and more sophisticated plans developed. In the late seventeenth century while the best houses in Edinburgh or Glasgow were built of stone, the majority were still constructed of timber. Many of the stone-constructed buildings had a timber front containing a covered passage on the ground floor serving as a pedestrian thoroughfare, with galleries on the upper floors. A characteristic building was the tall tenement; the product of an acute shortage of space making vertical expansion the only option open, they have a narrow plan built several storeys high. Another characteristic was the stone forestair rising directly from the street to join the principal tenement staircase.

The thriving trade with the Low Countries, the developing coastal trade and the abundance of freestone for building gave form and shape to the seaports of Fife. The most remarkable survival of this period is Culross. By-passed by the nineteenth-century industrialists it was, despite its small size, a flourishing port in the early seventeenth century. The houses, constructed of harled rubble with dressings to windows, doors and corners of yellow sandstone, rise two or three storeys. Upper floors are

Typical of the smaller towns and villages is this two-storey house with access by a forestair from the street, at Crail, Fife.

A new type of house, built in the early eighteenth century. Symmetrical in appearance it was built of two storeys with two rooms on each floor with fireplaces at the gable ends. This example comes from Falkland, Fife. As a house it suited a range of people – the merchants of the coastal ports, tacksmen, farmers, and others.

often reached by stone forestairs. The roofs are usually covered with pantiles, a product of trade with the Low Countries, while the gable ends of houses have the characteristic crow step.

A characteristic development in Stirling of the same period is the four-storey tenement buildings with circular stair towers projecting into the street. At Whithorn in the Wigtown District of Dumfries and Galloway Region, the plain two-storey houses are built of local flagstone rubble. Most are harled or colour-washed, while heavy stone slates are used as a roof cover. By the late seventeenth century stone was almost universal for building in the burghs while efforts were being made to prohibit thatch. Many houses were being rebuilt, windows were becoming larger as casement and sash windows gradually replaced the old traditional half-glazing of the sixteenth and seventeenth centuries, whereby the upper portion of the windows had glass set in fixed frames while shutters were provided for the lower portion.

By the end of the eighteenth century the farmer and his labourers, but rarely the shepherd, were living in better conditions. The new farmhouse, for the most part two storeys in height with a garret in the roof, usually formed one side of a farm court. They were oblong in shape, about 40 feet by 21 feet containing five rooms with additional accommodation for servants in the lofts. Under the agrarian reformers of the late eighteenth century many tenants were rehoused in stone-built houses with roofs covered in slate or pantiles. The one-storey cottages of the married labourers were much improved. Walls were about seven feet high and the floor was more often of flags or timber than earth. The roof was usually thatched but accommodation might include a kitchen, a bedroom for children and a garret. The theory behind such improvements was not entirely philanthropic. These improvements had to be paid for but the argument was put forward that well-housed tenants made better farmers than poorly-housed ones and so the expected higher profits would easily cover such developments. The architectural pattern books and agricultural journals were full of useful hints. Bricks were seldom used unless the laird, as in the Paxton district of Berwickshire, was prepared to support the establishment of a brick-and-tile works. One of the most notable of the village improvement schemes and also

Tenements for textile workers built at Blantyre, Lanark, Strathclyde Region. Notice how the external staircase turret of the Edinburgh tenements has been re-used here.

A late-eighteenth-century tacksman's house built at Ardlarach, Luing, Strathclyde Region

Eighteenth-century house at Kirk Yetholm,
Roxburgh, Borders Region

one of the earliest was Ormiston in East Lothian. It was begun 1734 by the local laird, the agricultural reformer John Cockburn. It was designed as the market centre for his estates as well as a thriving focus for rural industry in the locality. A brewery and distillery were founded and textile manufacture established.

Part of a group of three cottages built in 1755 at Tayinloan, Strathclyde Region

Nineteenth-century stone-built cottages, Dewarton, Midlothian

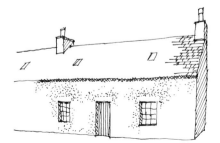

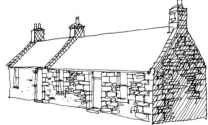

Above. *Eighteenth-century cottage at Lilliesleaf, Roxburgh, Borders Region. The walls are built of harled rubble.*

Below. *A cottage at Town Yetholm, Roxburgh, Borders Region, with harled rubble walls*

Most of the settlements continued the old traditions, using local materials and the well-tried methods of detail. The two-storey symmetrically-planned house modelled on the parish manse or smaller houses of the eighteenth century became standard, but the detached dwelling was too expensive to build and so the semi-detached house or long row or terrace of houses was developed. But some of the earliest improved cottages were a product of the period at the beginning of the Industrial Revolution. At Torbrex, in Stirling District in Central Region, there are some fine eighteenth-century weavers' houses while the weaving village of Carlops, in Tweedale in Borders Region, was founded by the local laird in 1784. The cottages, built in a row, consisted of a kitchen combined with a workshop but

Old Kilrenny Manse, Anstruther, Fife, dated 1590. Note the crow-stepped gables.

Adencaple House, Seil, Strathclyde Region. A laird's small house of the late eighteenth century. A symmetrically-planned building with a turnpike staircase built out in a semi-circular bay at the rear.

Residence of a tacksman, Cara, Strathclyde Region. It was built in 1733 of local rubble masonry laid in lime mortar. The roof is gable ended and slated.

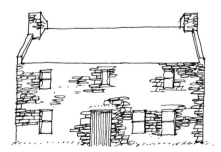

Weavers' cottages, Kilbarchan, Renfrew, Strathclyde Region. Advantage was taken of the sloping site to make an additional room above the weaving shop.

separated from a parlour by a through passage. The partition walls, known as Galashiels partition were constructed of panels of stone chippings set within strong timber frames. Most of these workers' houses were typical of the small, semi-industrial communities. At Chartershall, in Stirling, the nailmakers' houses of the late eighteenth century have a central entrance with a living room on either side. At the end of each house is a workshop with its own separate entrance.

Nailmakers' houses (1782), Chartershall, Stirlingshire, Central Region

Old houses at Causewayend, Ancrum, Roxburgh. These two-storeyed houses were built in the late eighteenth century. The walls are harled and the roofs covered in slate although one was originally thatched.

195

The little burgh of Gatehouse-of-Fleet once boasted a brewery, tannery, cotton mills, a boat-building yard and a bobbin factory. In the eighteenth century the laird canalized the River Fleet and the port of Gatehouse began to flourish, but during the following century industry began to recede from the Galloway towns. However seams of coal and iron ore in Strathclyde Region were being worked. In this area finer houses were made of granite while the small houses and cottages were built of whinstone, a hard sandstone, quarried from the lowland belt of grey-brown shale running right across Dumfries and Galloway.

The characteristic border country of Roxburgh, Selkirk and Peebles in the southeast Lowlands was almost unaffected by the Industrial Revolution since they had neither iron nor coal to export. But the border hills had long provided sheep runs and the weaving of tweeds was already an established tradition. Here, as in the north of England, the industry moved from the domestic economy of weavers working in their own cottages to the large-scale mills in Hawick, Galashiels, Walkerburn and Innerleithen.

While Central and West Fife concentrated on agriculture and coal mining during most of the Industrial Revolution nearly half the population of Scotland was centred in the Lowlands in and around the great Victorian city of Glasgow. The general adoption of coke fuel for smelting iron ore instead of charcoal during the latter part of the eighteenth century led to the large-scale establishment of the industry in the Central Lowlands where ironstone and coal were in abundance. The Carron Ironworks, established at Carron, in Stirling District in Central Region, in 1759 was planned to be the major iron-

Slate-quarrying workers' dwellings at Easdale, Seil, Strathclyde Region. These cottages were built in the nineteenth century; they consist of two rooms and the walls are of rubble masonry harled and whitewashed with roofs of slate.

196

Plan of cottage, Easdale, Strathclyde Region. A typical dwelling built for the workers in the local slate quarry. Built in 1856, each cottage has two main rooms separated by a lobby and closet.

Slate-quarry workers' dwellings built in the mid-seventeenth century of stone and lime, with slated roofs, at Ballachulish, Strathclyde Region

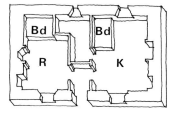

producing company in Britain. In 1779 a small coke furnace was built at Wilsontown, in the old county of Lanarkshire now in Strathclyde Region, while the Carron Company developed the nail trade at Cromond, Midlothian. They built industrial housing for the workers in the iron mills. During the same year the first effective cotton mill was established at Rothesay. Within a decade over twenty mills were in operation. The most important cotton-spinning centre was at New Lanark, in Strathclyde, founded by David Dale and Richard Arkwright in 1783. The manufacturing village they established was an experiment in community living controlled and managed by Dale's son-in-law, Robert Owen. Under Owen's far-sighted social experiments the Scots quickly became willing members of a community very foreign to their own.

Roads in the Lowlands were improved, canals built and, by the turn of the nineteenth century with the introduction of new machinery, the woollen trade, originally a domestic industry like the linen trade, became firmly established in the mills of Galashiels and Selkirk. Workers from Ireland and evicted crofters from the Highlands flocked to the

new industries. Despite the pioneering work at New Lanark, most of the new settlements planned for the increasing population of workers were not as original as many built in England. For the white-collar workers and the middle classes the remaining vestige of regional style was slowly swamped by more eclectic architectural styles. The model cottages of the pioneering industrial estates slowly gave way to Gothic cottages of suburbia and the bungalow of the twentieth century reigned supreme.

The new town of Cumbernauld, in the old county of Dunbartonshire and now in Strathclyde, tries to redress the balance. It was opened in 1967; it has one eye on the future and another on the past, but as far as the present is concerned the predominantly monotone aesthetics combined with the occasional coy picturesqueness seem to miss the point. The late-eighteenth-century planners and philanthropists were far better at it than the Cumbernauld Development Corporation. They stuck religiously to small planned settlements. Perhaps that is the answer. Maybe even their ingenuity would have failed with a town the size and complexity of Cumbernauld.

Plans and elevation of dwellings built for the workers at Lorn Furnace, Bonawe, Strathclyde Region in the late eighteenth century. All the buildings here are constructed of local rubble laid in lime mortar and the roofs are slated. This row of single-storeyed cottages, originally contained a single living room with a loft above, reached by means of a steep timber staircase opening off a small entrance lobby.

These dwellings were built to house the workers employed at Lorn Furnace. The furnace was established in 1753 by a group of Lakeland ironmasters, with the object of utilizing locally-produced charcoal to smelt haematite ore brought in by sea from Lancashire and Cumbria. The furnace was finally closed down in 1874.

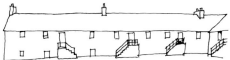

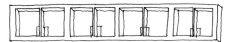

First floor

Ground floor

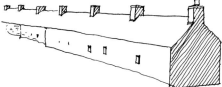

Workers' dwellings, Port Ramsay, Lismore, Strathclyde Region. Single-storey cottages of rubble masonry with limewashed walls and slate roofs. Built at the turn of the nineteenth century.

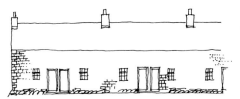

The Scottish Highlands and Islands

The character of most Highland houses was formed by the fierce Atlantic winds and storms that each building was designed to keep out, while the nature and extent of materials available gave them style. For obvious reasons little was imported. Before 1800 most of the rural labourers and artisans in the forested districts of Inverness, in Highland Region, lived in some form of primitive timber-framed building. In the treeless outer islands, before the era of the lighthouse, the numerous ships wrecked along the coast cast ashore an ample supply of timber for the roof timbers of houses. Many houses in Tiree have such roof timbers.

The typical form of construction was the use of crucks or couples, as they are known in Scotland. Most crucks were single blades of timber, but in Skye and the western Highlands many couples are jointed at wall-head level, the lower blade being scarfed and pegged to the upper one. Numerous examples of cruck-framed buildings survive in the central and western Highlands and in southwest Scotland. Up to the end of the eighteenth century many of these buildings were walled with wattle and turf while roofs

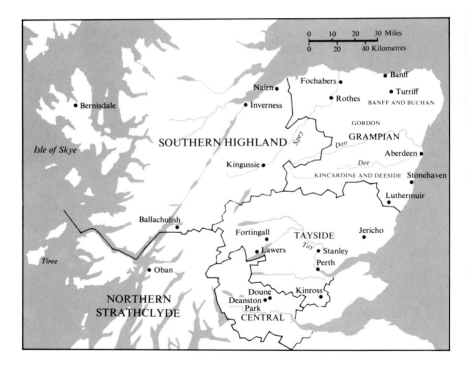

Previous page. *The harbour at Stonehaven, Grampian. The houses have the typical neat but austere façades.*

were covered with branches and turf and then thatched.

Genuine black houses are found today only in the outer isles, but in Skye there is a variation of the typical black houses of the Hebrides. Here the characteristic detail is the hip-ended roof and the overhanging eaves of thatch. The older plans included house and byre under one roof. The fire was in an open hearth with a small smoke vent above. One end of the black house is always higher than the other. The byre was at the lower end. In the earlier days there was no partition between the byre where the cattle were

Skye type of black house with hipped ends to the roof and overhanging eaves. Nineteenth-century engraving.

There are two types of black house found in
this area of Scotland–the Skye type (as seen
below) and the Dalriadic type (illustrated on
page 208). The Skye type has a hipped-end roof
of thatch with overhanging eaves. The Dalriadic
type has overhanging eaves, like the Skye type,
but only front and back.

The end walls are gabled. The thatch was
lashed to the roof, transversely and longitu-
dinally, by straw ropes. The ends of the
horizontal ropes were tied to the edge of the
gable wall by pins. The same method was used
along the eaves, although stone weights were
often used.

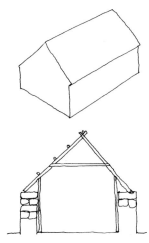

The Skye type of black house usually consists of
two rooms, byre and house, open to the roof. The
central fire was originally an open hearth. The
fireplaces and chimneys were added later.
Windows were few and small. The byre was
later converted into a living room, the animals
being housed in an attached byre. Later still a
third room was added to the plans while a
porch was built as a draught lobby to some of
the houses.

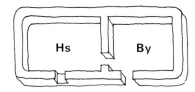

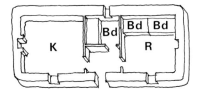

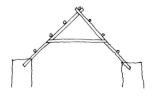

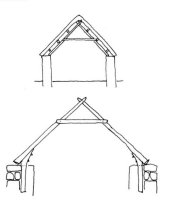

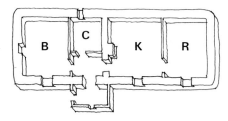

kept and the living room, and men attempted to shut out the cow from a view of the fire. A partition was eventually erected and then, later still, the byre was built as a separate building. The revised house plan then consisted of an entry door centred in the long wall. At one end would be the kitchen, at the other a large room and the two were divided by an entry hall and a closet, large enough to accommodate a bed. A fireplace was usually built into each end wall, the short chimney just protruding above the ridge. In some houses the fireplace and chimney were placed on the internal cross wall. A distinctive characteristic is the way in which the thatch is dressed and bound around the protruding chimney. In some houses the hanging chimney is more common; here the flue was made of a wood box. It was enlarged to make a hood over the hearth and the whole chimney was fixed to the wall.

Where more space was needed, rooms were added on the kitchen end. Sometimes a storm porch would be built to cover the entrance from draughts. The walls were built of undressed stone. Most corners were rounded, but where dressed stone was available the corners were squared. Most roof trusses were of the collar-beam type, while branches with a bed of turf and thatch formed the roof cover, the eaves extending over the external wall. The thatch was roped and weighted by stones tied just above the eaves or hanging down the face of the wall. Later the ropes were replaced by wire netting. The stones were suspended from the wire netting by hoops of wire. Windows set deep in the wall were usually arranged symmetrically on either side of the entrance door. Floors were normally of beaten earth, but some cottages had wooden floors. Most rooms were open to the roof rafters, but later ceilings were

installed. Internal walls were whitewashed or lined with wood boarding covered with paper.

Another variation of the black house, found in the former county of Argyll now in Strathclyde, and West Perth and Kinross in Tayside Region, differs little in plan but is distinguished by end walls carried up to the ridge of the roof to form a gable. But, like the black houses of Skye, the thatch is carried over the front edge of the house to form overhanging eaves. Roof pitches were fairly steep, and fireplaces and chimneys were built on to the end walls.

Black house, Isle of Skye

Black house, Isle of Skye. Note how the chimney was added later along the end wall.

*Cottage of random rubble walling and
pantiled roof at Doune, Perth, Tayside Region*

*Crofter's cottage on the Isle of Skye, Highlands
Region*

207

The Dalriadic type of black house has more conspicuous windows. The stone walls are usually about two feet or more in thickness, the stones roughly dressed to provide square corners, jambs and lintels. A characteristic feature is the use of the backs of box beds to form a partition between lobby and kitchen; the door of the kitchen was placed between the ends of the box beds.

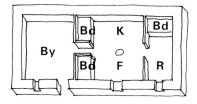

Dalriadic type of black house, Isle of Mull

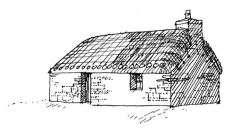

Dalriadic type of black house, Isle of Skye

Windows were characterized by large lintels. Some houses had ceilings and lofts. The cross wall in the kitchen was usually formed by a double box bed, with a central entry hall and closet and a further room beyond. This gable-ended cottage was universally popular and is found in most parts of the Highlands.

Places affect people and people affect places. It is difficult to say how much of the highly distinctive character of the Highlander was shaped and moulded by the bleak mountains and isolated glens of the remote northwest. One can clearly see, however, how the Celts themselves adapted to their environment. They did not tend to build towns or cities but lived in extended communities or clans held together by family ties and by loyalty to their chiefs, to whom indeed most of them were highly conscious of being related, however remotely. So closely knit were the communities of these mountain refuges and offshore islands that, until the present century, they preserved an older way of life that had long since disappeared from the more accessible Lowlands. They lived by cattle droving, by following their chiefs in war and by hunting. Agriculture and fisheries were not highly cultivated, while crofting and sea fishing, which still sustain those who live in the remoter parts today, are more recent developments.

Cattle rearing dominated the Highland economy in the early seventeenth century. Until the mid-nineteenth century great herds of cattle were driven annually to the markets of the Scottish Lowlands. During the more stable times preceding the Jacobite Rebellion the population, freed from smallpox following the developments in vaccination by Edward Jenner in 1798, increased rapidly. The division of crofts resulted in more and more people occupying smaller holdings.

Crofters had no security of tenure. The land was owned by a laird or else held on a long lease or tack by a tacksman or gentleman farmer to whom the crofter paid rent and services. When the clearance began in earnest in the first half of the nineteenth century, the crofter had no protection. In the South and Central Highlands new crop rotations brought the need for enclosure, and with the inevitable introduction of long leases the old tacksmen and their joint tenants were replaced by individual farmers.

The destruction of the clan system had disintegrated a social system. Lairds who had been drawn into metropolitan life needed cash and their link with the common Islesman was at best tenuous or even broken by this time. It was dis-covered that the hardy sheep of the border country could be kept out all the year on the northern hills. There was a great demand for wool and large profits to be made. Cattle had enriched the land, their grass grazings extended far out into the moorlands for their cropping of coarser grass gave life to finer grass. But sheep could be raised with less labour than cattle, and soon they were introduced to the Central Highlands and western mainlands. There was at this time a surplus population. Some found employment on the new sheep farms while the rest, in some areas entire communities of crofters, were cleared off the land between 1820 and 1840. Many emigrated while others eked out a living on the wastelands along the coast.

Improvements were made to houses by inserting a ceiling of oak branches covered with turf

The later plan, minus the byre, was the prototype for the simple Highland cottage

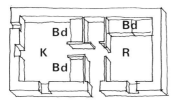

Auchanachy Castle, Grampian Region, built in the sixteenth century. Even the great house has the same austere and spartan appearance in its detailing, use of materials and simplicity of plan. The work of the architect Mackintosh, as seen at Windy Hill House, Kilmacolm near Glasgow (1899–1901) is a link between this and the simplicity and order of the crofter's cottage.

Rethatching at Fortingall, Perth, Tayside

In the northwest Highlands and islands the growth of the kelpmaking industry in the mid-eighteenth century provided considerable employment. Fishing provided an alternative income when the kelp industry declined in the 1830s, but the disastrous famine after the potato blight of 1846 and the ensuing years, was followed by a decline of the west-coast fishing industry which merely worsened the crofters' plight. Sheep farming by now was no longer yielding the same profits as it had in earlier years. The once rich pasture had been cropped so short that it left only rough grass and bracken to spread and by the late nineteenth century the land was given over to deer.

The conditions of the crofters were such that, in Skye in 1882, many crofters resisted the process of eviction by the local sheriff's officers. An absurdly nervous government at Westminster sent up a man-o'-war to sort out the problem. A commission of inquiry was set up which resulted in the Crofters Holding Act of 1886 giving the crofters security of tenure,

grants for improvements and fair rents.

The stone used to build the traditional black houses was not always readily available. Clay had been used as a filler for slate and wattle walls and for wattle chimney hoods, but in seventeenth-century Aberdeenshire, now part of Grampian Region, mud walling was used not only for building the humble cottages but for the building of manses, churches and town houses. Clay was mixed with straw and the walls built up like the cob cottages of Devon. But at the vulnerable points, such as the sides of doors and windows and the corners of houses, hewn stone was used where possible. The walls were built in courses of varying depth and thickness. Where the roof was supported by cruck trusses or a framed structure, the walls were non-loadbearing and less substantial, but where loads had to be carried then the courses were made lower and thicker. The walls were usually built on stone or cobble footings which acted as a kind of damp-proof course.

In Moray most clay buildings were

Nineteenth-century house with peat stack, Bernisdale, Skye. The peat stack is the darker mound to the left of the drawing. Note the thatching taken up around the chimney; also the hipped ends to the roof, typical of black houses on Skye.

Range of single-unit houses, built in the late eighteenth century at Lawers, Tayside Region

confined to towns but in the countryside of Nairn, Banff and Buchan, and Gordon the better houses were made of stone while the humbler dwellings were of turf daubed with clay plaster or alternating layers of turf and stone. In parts of Moray, and Banff and Buchan clay was mixed with sand and straw. This mixture, combined with large stones, was used in the construction of many houses built in the towns of Banff, Aberdeen and Turriff in the late nineteenth century. The first houses of the clay city in Luthermuir, in Kincardine and Deeside, in Grampian Region, were built by squatters from the clay beneath their feet. It was begun in the late eighteenth century and was occupied mainly by handloom weavers by the mid-nineteenth century. In parts of the old county of Perthshire, now in Tayside Region, most buildings were built of clay while in the northeast of Scotland, particularly between Fife and Moray, clay thatching was a particular feature at this time. The thatch was laid in a vertical course from eaves to ridge and then clayed over before the second course was laid into position.

Many of the houses of the east-coast towns exhibit the roll-moulded surrounds, crow-stepped gables and angle turrets typical of the seventeenth century. Walls were often built of granite while roofs were usually of stone slates. Some mid-eighteenth-century houses were built of blocks of peat, stone and broom, and some town houses had their street façades especially stuccoed or rubble faced. Arbroath, a prosperous manufacturing centre of the late eighteenth century, has some attractive colour-washed houses with the characteristic forestairs.

A primitive form of iron smelting had been carried on in many parts of Scotland since early times, but it was the establishment of the Invergarry furnace in 1727 that brought the Industrial Revolution to the Highlands. Wood for furnace charcoal was almost impossible to obtain but the Highlands had plenty, so ore was shipped from the Lancashire and Cumbrian mines. The smelted pig iron was returned southwards.

The linen trade was essentially domestic until well into the nineteenth century, but with the introduction of machine spinning, it established itself firmly in Fife, Perth and Kinross, and Angus.

By the late eighteenth century the cotton industry was firmly established in Perth and Kinross District at the Stanley Cotton Mills. Housing was scarce, and a model industrial village of two-storeyed houses of stone and brick was built in 1785. But by the second half of the eighteenth century many Scottish landowners had become convinced of the need to found village communities, partly to stimulate trade and partly to resettle the rural population displaced by the changing agrarian economy. Fochabers, in the District of Moray in Grampian

One-and-a-half-storey type housing in the planned village of Rothes, Grampian Region, built in 1766. Note the characteristic stone gabled dormers of this type of terrace housing.

View of Oban, Argyll, in 1857. The simplicity and austerity of the compact regular new settlements was a continuation of the building tradition of the region.

Region, was a replanned village of whitewashed housing built round a large market square in the late eighteenth century. It was built by the 4th Duke of Gordon and replaced an earlier village which had been removed when the castle was extended. The industrial housing of Deanston Park in Perthshire, Central, was built in the late eighteenth century for Buchanan and Arkwright. The houses were again white-washed giving a clean and cheerful aspect, and each was provided with a garden.

The influx of workers into highly-concentrated areas where housing was already at a premium created much misery and considerable hardship. Many of the more fervent village planners saw the immorality that they believed such conditions bred being tempered by the clean lines and ordered atmosphere of the new settlements. The main essentials were

convenient sites with a good water supply, building materials and transport, and a flexible plan, easy to extend. As one planner, the Reverend Robert Rennie, pointed out in the early nineteenth century the concept behind the plan was that it should have the appearance of a complete village, however small, or a compact regular town, however enlarged, and this concept was conformed to during the development of many of the unplanned villages and towns of the Highlands. The model villages here, although not always as dramatic, are probably the few in the British Isles to be infused with any real kind of life, or, rather, infused with the kind of life the people locally are prepared to live. Houses are orderly and utilitarian, the materials limited without being dull, and the major part of the village ensemble conforms without being uniform.

Northern Scotland

Of all the Highland areas of Scotland, the island of Lewis is the last to retain the seasonal migration of herds from a winter settlement to summer pastures. This practice, which allowed the grazing lands of the winter settlement to recover while giving cattle the benefit of the fresh hill pastures, was once widespread throughout the highland areas of Europe. On the mainland the herdsmen built shielings for shelter on the summer pastures frequently constructed of turf and wattle, here, in the Western Isles they were built of a dry-stone wall of boulders. The walls,

usually about five feet in thickness, consisted of two layers of stone with an infilling of earth. The roof was covered in turf. The basic plans differed little to the shielings of Cumbria, but the older shielings used until the beginning of the nineteenth century were generally circular in plan with a dome-shaped roof of corbelled stone. This technique of construction recalls the early Christian oratories of Scotland and Ireland. In some instances these beehive shielings, as they are referred to in this area, were grouped together to form a complex of

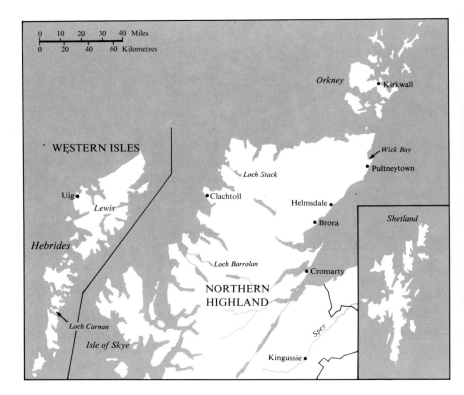

Previous page. *A croft beside Loch Barrolan at Altnacealgach, Sutherland*

linked apartments. The construction of the corbelled-stone roof limited the size of shielings to less than fourteen feet. As larger rooms were required the rectangular plan with a timber roof became common.

The winter settlements were much more substantial affairs, but here again, the nature of materials available, the harshness of the climate and the general economy of the land largely fashioned the crofts in the austere and utilitarian manner seen today. The croft is a tiny farm, often less than five acres in size.

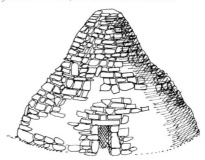

Beehive huts, Isle of Lewis. This reconstruction is typical of the beehive huts of the Bronze Age, (1800–500 B.C.). This type of hut was found in Wales, Cornwall and Scotland.

Beehive huts at Uig, Lewis. They were still inhabited in 1859.

The austerity in building is in keeping with the mountain solitude beside Loch Stack, Sutherland

Most of the Hebridean black houses are planned as a long oblong divided into three rooms. The entrance door led directly through the byre to the house. Many houses on the Isle of Lewis were planned with two or three buildings joined along their sides.

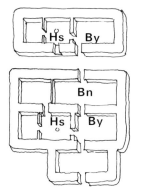

Section through black houses made of three buildings on Lewis

Triple combination, Lewis

Twin combination, Lewis

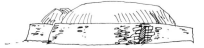

Here the crofter and his family could earn a bare but basic living, supplemented by fishing, weaving or possibly building roads in the area.

The numerous bays and inlets of Lewis and Harris made excellent harbours for small boats and ideal sites for tiny villages. Inshore fishing was good in a hinterland studded with trout lochs. But the lack of soil made it necessary for the crofters to make their own soil for tillage. In the hollows of the rocks, selected because of the good drainage, they built up platforms of peat. Across this platform they spread seaweed which they had carried up in creels from the shore. On these beds, or lazybeds as they are called, they planted potatoes and oats.

This is the traditional way of life in the Highlands and islands. In Sutherland most of the inhabitants are crofters. Here the proportion of arable land is the lowest in Scotland, with much of the area given over to sheep runs and deer forests. It was here that the Norsemen were dominant between the eleventh and thirteenth centuries.

Caithness offers more promise to the farmer than Sutherland despite the wide tracts of moorland suitable only for game or for grazing. Fishing, the second main industry, provides the necessary supplementary income. The richest arable land is found in Orkney and the Orcadians are famous farmers; they are a self-contained and prosperous people. Whereas the Shetlander is said to be a sailor and fisherman who has a small croft, the Orcadian is said to be a farmer who has a boat.

*A croft by the shore of Loch Carnan, South
Uist. A chimney and wider windows were
added to a traditional Skye type of black house.*

Most of the buildings seen today were built comparatively recently. Earlier dwellings of a fairly rudimentary nature had a short life. In some areas where timber was particularly scarce it was customary for the tenants when they moved from farm to farm to take the roof timbers with them.

There are numerous cruck-framed buildings in Scotland. Most have gable ends of stone or clay. In some of the more recent buildings the crucks themselves have been raised off the ground and rested on wall plates on a low wall. In the far north, in the old counties of Sutherland and Caithness in Highland Region, timber was scarce so many crucks had to be made up of old ships' timbers. In the late eighteenth century many of the houses in Sutherland were still walled with sods, while partition walls were usually of wattle daubed with clay. But the most characteristic house in the area is the Hebridean black house. The landscape in part of the Western Isles is dotted with these long low dry-stone buildings, nestling in the fold of the brae. They probably owe their name to the fact that there was no chimney to allow the escape of smoke from the central peat fire. As it slowly found its way out through what openings were available, the smoke gradually blackened most of the interior.

The characteristic features were a roof thatched with heather and weighted down with boulders, a byre leading off the living quarters and enormously thick walls of dry-stone walling. By the late nineteenth century many were replaced by the more superior white houses, again built by the crofters themselves. The white houses had chimneys, the stone walls were cemented together, and some roofs were covered in slate.

The black houses were designed to

A black house from the Isle of Lewis, rebuilt at Kingussie, Highlands Region

Black house of the Hebridean type

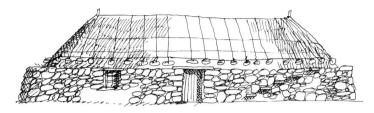

Aerial view of the Hebridean type of black house. The characteristic feature is the exposed broad ledge of wall top which extends around the house.

cope with the fierce Atlantic winds and to stand up to the frequent winter hurricanes, so the thick dry-stone walls have neither corners nor gables. Although black houses are a characteristic of Skye as well, a distinguishing feature of those built in Lewis, Harris, and the outer islands is the exposed broad ledge of wall top which extends around the house. In Tiree these walls vary in thickness up to nine feet, but the average wall is six feet thick and about six feet high. The stones for the walls were in the form of boulders of which there was an abundance in the hillsides. The walls are built of two separate walls with a two-foot-wide space between them. The outer wall face is sloped inwards. The space itself is filled with earth or gravel to form a hearting or core. The roof was raised on the inner face of the wall to avoid eaves. The part of the top left exposed was then turfed over. Sheep or lambs would often be found grazing on the wall top. Frequently the roof had to be rethatched. Few crofters had ladders so, in order to make it easier to climb to the wall top, steps were

occasionally formed in the wall by projecting stones.

Unlike many earth-filled cavity walls, the central hearting of earth or gravel was used neither for construction purposes nor for achieving greater thicknesses in walling. Rainwater discharged from the roof on to the wall top would then percolate through the hearting to the soil. The damp blanket of earth thus formed would prevent the fierce Atlantic winds from penetrating the uncemented masonry of the wall. The boulders of the inner wall were canted upwards, forming a primitive kind of vertical damp-proof course to prevent any of this moisture reaching the interior.

The traditional plan, typical of Orkney and Shetland farmhouses, is a long rectangle divided into three rooms. The main entrance was usually through the byre at the lower end. The byre was separated from the domestic quarters of the house by a stone cross wall and interconnecting door. Originally this separation was made by a simple stone kerb and timber screen. The central room

was the kitchen-living room, while the third compartment forming a bedroom was separated from the main room by a wooden partition. But later the byre was built as a separate detached dwelling and the entrance door to the dwelling house itself was positioned centrally along one of the side walls. On the island of Lewis a more rudimentary form of black house was built of three irregularly-shaped buildings joined together. On one end was the barn with its own rear entrance. An internal door connected the barn to the central unit which was composed of a byre and kitchen-living room. The main entrance was through a combined porch and stable. Sometimes a store room was built off the kitchen. In some of the larger farms in Orkney, numerous outhouses were built in a row, forming a wall of buildings parallel with the farmhouse.

Roofs were constructed of the collar-beam type of roof truss. The rafters formed a fork at the ridge while the feet of the truss were fixed on the inner part of the wall. A characteristic of the black houses of Tiree in Strathclyde is the flatly rounded ridge formed by fixing a curved piece of timber to the top ends of the rafters. Occasionally, radiating rafters were used to form rounded ends.

A cover of branches was laid across the roof timbers. These were then covered with sods of turf to form a bed for the thatch. In order to secure the thatch from the Atlantic winds the roof covering was roped down with heather and the ropes were tied to stones. For additional security, horizontal ropes were interlaced with vertical ropes. When roofs needed rethatching it was carried out during the summer months. The smoke-saturated thatch which was taken off was often used as a fertilizer.

The peat fire was originally lit in a central stone hearth, the smoke either drifting out through the thatched roof or through a smoke hole. Later the hearth was moved to the end walls and a chimney built. The floor of the house was invariably of beaten earth. In order to accommodate the manure, the byre floor was set lower than that of the living room. When sufficient manure had accumulated it was removed and then used as a fertilizer for the crops. There were no windows in the older houses. Later a skylight was occasionally formed in the thatched roof. Where windows were formed, they were deeply set with reveals of four feet or more in breadth. The sill was built of rubble or glass, while large stones were used for the jambs at the side of the window. In some of the older houses a bed recess was built within the thickness of the walls. In Orkney many beds were accommodated in small projecting alcoves, while on the mainland timber box beds were common in the eighteenth and early nineteenth centuries.

The crofting townships of Lewis and Harris, which spread up the west coast, lie on a mile-wide strip between moorland,

227

road and sea. The more recently-built white houses are two storeys in height, of grey-cemented walls and roofs covered in corrugated iron, bitumen felt or asbestos tile. Most of the old black houses are now used as byres or weaving sheds, but some have been modernized. Beside each house are huge stacks of peat which also form useful windbreaks. Most of the houses in Lewis are stark and unpainted. Today many crofters are involved in weaving tweeds for transport to the mills at Stornoway.

In this comparatively spartan area the local building tradition has been retained and much of its original character can be seen. The greatest changes occurred during the notorious Highland clearances, sparked off by the Jacobite Rebellion of 1745. In an attempt to smoke out this rebellious area the government did its best to destroy the Highland tradition. The Highlanders were disarmed, their national dress prohibited and Gaelic made a shameful tongue. Whichever side the Highlander had taken he was made to feel inferior to the English. This was followed by the anti-Gael, anti-Celt policy of the Highland clearances. There were various reasons for the tragedy, many originating in events before the '45, but it was the '45 that accelerated the disaster. Many Highlanders, seeing greater profits in sheep farming, began to evict their clansmen. Later the moorlands and mountainsides were turned into great sporting grounds. These clearances lasted until the late nineteenth century when a series of Crofters Acts were passed protecting the rights of the Highland peasant.

Typical burgh houses of the late sixteenth and seventeenth centuries are to be found at Kirkwall in Orkney. Most are built of local flagstone laid in clay mortar

and roofed with heavy stone slates. The house fronts are narrow and they are also usually gabled.

Cromarty Harbour which had been destroyed by the sea was rebuilt in the late eighteenth century by the local laird, George Ross, to serve his newly-established hempen-cloth factory. This sudden prosperity is reflected in the more spacious two- and three-storey town houses. The fairly plain houses built of red-sandstone rubble are occasionally

Plan and elevation of a typical improved cottage of the mid-nineteenth century. This box-like dwelling was typical of many illustrated in the pattern books of the period.

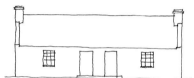

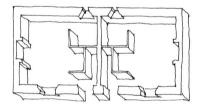

An early-nineteenth-century crofter's house in Clachtoll, Sutherland. This is a development of the Dalriadic type of black house. Fireplaces were built at both gable ends.

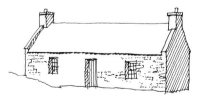

characterized by rusticated quoins and the provision of a radial fanlight over the entrance doors.

By the early nineteenth century there was a considerable amount of building. The Marquess of Stafford built two ports in Sutherland. One, Brora, now a holiday centre, was built between 1811 and 1813 as a coal-mining and salt-producing centre. The other was Helmsdale, a herring and fishing port founded in 1814. Each was laid out on a regular grid plan. The Marquess of Stafford, one of the largest landowners in the Highlands, had been severely criticized for his behaviour during the clearances. The two ports were, if anything, a belated attempt to exonerate himself. Skilled craftsmen were introduced to teach new trades, bricks and tiles were manufactured on the estate for the vast building programme, while the improved house designs began revolutionizing standards of rural and urban housing in this part of Scotland.

Standard layouts were developed and financial inducements were offered to workers for the most soundly-built dwellings. Numerous ideas were developed in pattern books concerning improved cottages for the labouring classes. Many of these trim one-storey cottages proposed were built on numerous estate villages.

Perhaps the most interesting of all was the model fishing town of Pultneytown on the south side of the river running into Wick Bay, Caithness. The town was founded in the early nineteenth century by the British Fisheries Society. The plan prepared by Thomas Telford, was finally carried out in 1830. There was a mixture of one- and two-storey houses, a small number of which had spacious attics designed to accommodate fishing gear. House plans were simple and utilitarian, the house façades neat but austere and this building tradition is still flourishing in many parts of northern Scotland.

Ireland

From the Middle Ages until the mid-nineteenth century one of the main characteristics of the predominantly pastoral economy of Ireland was the summer migration of herdsmen and their families to the lusher pastures in the mountains as was the tradition in the rest of Europe. Similar to many nomadic herdsmen, they travelled considerable distances from their winter settlements

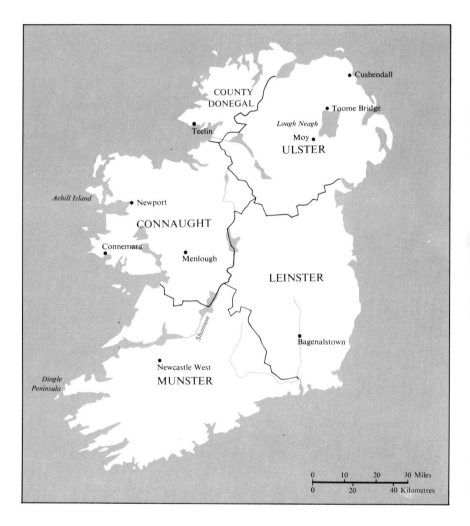

Previous page. *A cottage in Connemara, County Galway. The thatch is secured by ropes and the ropes are pegged to the gable walls and the top of the main walls along the eaves. Large boulders form the base of the walls.*

and needed to build some kind of rudimentary shelter; these were known as booleys and they are not unlike the shielings of Northumberland and Cumbria. They were usually built of sods on a foundation of earth and stone. Some were built of stone when it was available as in Achill Island, County Mayo. They consisted of one large room, either oval in plan or rectangular with rounded corners. They varied in size, the average room being about 10 feet by 20 feet. In the bogland areas, they were built into a sloping bank of peat or gravel. The roofs were constructed of bog timbers and covered by long strips of sod and thatched with heather secured by ropes. There were no windows and usually only one door opening positioned in one of the long walls. Occasionally a second door would be made in the long wall opposite. The fire was placed in an open hearth along one of the walls.

Their winter home, the bally, was a slightly more substantial dwelling built of clay or loose stones with green sods as a filler for the gaps. Shelter from the prevailing winds was essential, the result being groups of between twenty and sixty houses arranged in a disorderly cluster. This small settlement, usually called a clachan, had none of the features of the traditional village such as a church, inn or shops. The houses were small, usually one storey in height, rectangular in plan and never more than one room in width.

A characteristic feature in the north and west was the presence of a front and a back door, each one opposite the other. This was possibly a means of regulating the draught from the open fire, much like the positioning of windows in the medieval Welsh hall house. When chimney flues were added the back door was often blocked up or turned into a window or cupboard. Where a byre was included

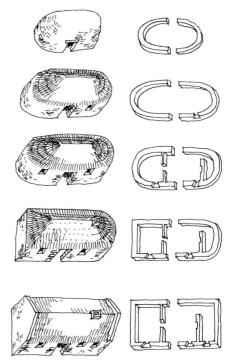

Five stages in the development of the traditional house in western Ireland from the primitive clochan to the present-day house. Note how the gable end finally replaced the hipped roof.

Plan of a small house in west County Limerick. The entrance door is positioned away from the hearth. Originally there would have been a door opposite, as in houses in southwest County Donegal. This was probably blocked up. House plans with an entrance door of this relationship to the hearth are typical of the mountain area of south County Dublin and County Wicklow.

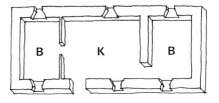

under the same roof, then the second door was retained and the passage served as a path for livestock as well. In many rural areas this was the traditional type of dwelling. Many had rounded ends and hipped roofs. Later the gabled house was typical in most of western Ireland. Fires were burned in the traditional central hearth which acted as a room divider. Some of the more substantial houses had at least three rooms. At Menlough, in northeast Galway, the house walls, built of local limestone, are two to three feet thick. Roofs are thatched with sedge from the nearby lake. The open-field form of farming predominated in these areas, although a few people specialized in weaving and thatching.

The basic form of the traditional Irish house differs little. Most, particularly in the rural areas, consisted of a series of rooms each opening into the next while roofs, determined by a predominantly rainy climate and also the nature of straw and reed which is used as a roof covering, are steeply pitched. The major differences occur in shape and detail, the most important influences being the availability of materials and building expertise which, in their turn, were governed largely by political, social and economic constraints.

Thatched and hip-roofed farmhouse built in the early nineteenth century at Corradreenan, West townland, County Fermanagh.

Cottier's or labourer's dwelling from Duncrun townland, north County Derry, built about 1750. Notice the simplicity between this house and the Dalriadic type of house so typical of the Highlands of Scotland. The chimney is a hole in the roof.

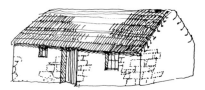

A house on Achill Island, County Mayo. Notice the crow-stepped stone gables.

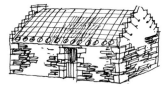

A plan of a large farmhouse in County Wexford. This house plan is typical of many in South Leinster and East Munster.

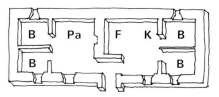

Right. *A typical thatched and rubble-walled cottage in Connemara, County Galway*

By the time Cromwell had butchered his way through much of Ireland, famine, plague and the sword had reduced the population to just over half a million in the mid-seventeenth century. The Catholic Church was suppressed and many Irish emigrated, while Protestants, encouraged with gifts of land, began to colonize the towns and countryside. They began to dominate not only the landowning classes, but also the urban, commercial, industrial and professional life of the country. The restoration of Charles II in 1660 merely confirmed Cromwellian settlers in power and possession.

Under James II, Catholic rights were restored while Parliament, with its Catholic majority, began to restore the lands confiscated by Cromwell. The northern Protestants, fearing for both their rights and privileges, sided with the Williamite rebellion which broke out in England and soon engulfed Ireland. After the Williamite victory at Aughrim in 1691 land was again confiscated and by 1700 only one-seventh of the land remained in Catholic ownership. The Catholic

majority was deprived of its political and civil rights. In Ulster custom gave the Presbyterian tenant rights denied his Catholic neighbour. When leases were renewed Catholics had little choice but to attempt to outbid the Presbyterian tenant, and this, of course, suited the unscrupulous landlords. The inevitable outcome of this was sectarian conflict which coupled with wholesale rent raising in 1718, resulted in mass emigration to New England.

A century later the close of the Napoleonic Wars brought widespread poverty, unemployment and eviction. The famines in 1817 and 1821 together with a growing population, harassment by landlords and the resulting counteraction from the poor, led to more oppression. The final catastrophe was the Great Famine of 1846–8. Hundreds of thousands perished of hunger and cholera while others fled to Britain or America. But the very poor could not flee because they did not have the means. The following decades brought further distress for them: more unemployment and wholesale evictions. Most were lucky to have a roof over their heads, no matter how insubstantial. Rarely had they the means for much else even in more affluent times. The rudimentary buildings of the bally and booley system must have seemed a luxury to them.

The cruck-framed structure, perhaps the most common form of building for the peasant in medieval England, is comparatively rare in Ireland. It was confined primarily to the northwest. The roofs were thatched, the walls built of solid clay or of wattle and daub. Timber-framed houses, numerous in the medieval

Section through an old house in County Armagh. The coupled rafters are carried on uprights positioned in the mud walls.

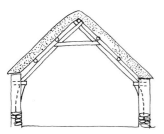

Left. *Whitewashed cottage near Newport, County Mayo*

*There are only three basic plan types of the
traditional Irish house. The major variations
are to be found in the different elements which
make up the house, such as a roof form,
construction and covering, hearth and chimney,
the outshut, materials and building methods.*
*a. Two-roomed house found largely in eastern
and southeastern Ireland.*
*b. A house on Dingle Peninsula, County
Kerry. This is a house with two outside doors
opposite each other, a wooden or furniture
partition between kitchen and bedroom. It is
common in West Ulster, Connaught and West
Munster.*
*c. This house, also typical in Scotland has
chimneys at each gable end. It is common in
northeastern Ireland.*

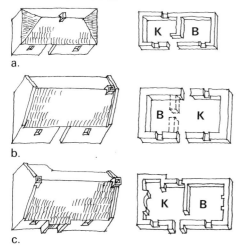

*Plan and elevation of typical farmhouse of
southwest County Donegal. The long rectangular plan is broken by the bed alcove beside
the kitchen hearth.*

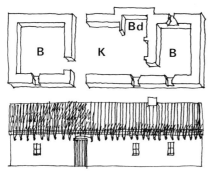

towns, were still being built in the
plantation villages of Ulster in the
seventeenth century but the general
levelling of the woods during the unending succession of wars, revolts and
clearances coupled with the prodigal use
of timber for ship building and the iron
industry, so denuded the forests of
Ireland during the sixteenth, seventeenth
and eighteenth centuries that little was
left for building. The lack of timber,
particularly for longer spans, restricted
the width of rooms. Houses which needed
extending did so lengthwise. Solid walls
of stone or clay therefore became more
characteristic.

There are three basic types of houses.
One, rectangular in shape, consisted of a
central open hearth which when a
protecting wall was built around one side
of the hearth, divided the houses into two
compartments: a living-kitchen room and
a bedroom. In the second type the hearth
was moved to the end wall. Control of
draughts was necessary and a back and
front door were built opposite each other.
There was still a living-kitchen room,
while the bedroom was formed behind a
partition of heavy furniture consisting of
a dresser or cupboard. The third type,
found chiefly in the northeast, has a
fireplace at each end. The introduction of
chimney flues meant that double doors
could be dispensed with. The one door
opened into the living-kitchen room. The
bedroom was to one side behind a solid
wall. In a corner of the main room in
many parts of Ireland a bed boxed in with
timber framing was common. In parts of
Ulster and northwest Connaught a
typical feature was the bed built in a
recess projecting out from the house. In
this same region the byre, included under
the same roof, formed the traditional
longhouse. The back and front door were
usually retained. The cow entered by the

The interior of a kitchen in a hill farm from Coscib townland, near Cushendall, County Antrim. The main entrance is in the furthest corner from the fireplace. Most of the furniture was pushed against the walls leaving the main floor area free.

front door but after milking it was led out through the back door while another was brought in at the front. In some parts of northwest Ulster, particularly along the Atlantic seaboard of County Donegal, many houses with byres were built down a steep slope. The upper or hearth end was built into the bank while the lower end, with side walls over twelve feet high, could be lofted over. Cattle were housed in the byre on the ground floor with a bedroom built above it. The bedroom and kitchen were on split levels. Where the cross passage in the traditional longhouse would have been, a ladder or stone steps were built to reach the bedroom. Both kitchen and bedroom were open to the roof rafters.

The kitchen of a farmhouse from
Corradreenan West townland, County
Fermanagh. The original chimney of clay-
plastered wickerwork was replaced in the
nineteenth century by this substantial brick
chimney.

Plan and perspective section of house with two
bedrooms over the byre and service room on
Gola Island.

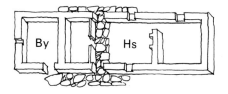

By   Hs

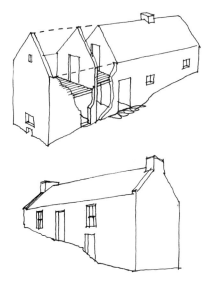

A house with the bedroom over the byre in
County Donegal

The interior of the kitchen in a cottier's house from Duncrun townland, North Derry. A characteristic feature is the bed recess built in an outshut in a corner of the kitchen. The floor is earthen; the chimney canopy consists of wattlework plastered with clay or mud and whitewashed.

Glass for windows was a luxury. In the humbler dwellings windows usually positioned away from the prevailing winds were few and small. Things changed little in the nineteenth century when a window tax was levied. A typical feature was the half-door, the lower half was closed while the top half admitted light.

Since timber, apart from bog oak, was so scarce, most builders had to resort to stone, clay, sods, grass and straw. The most primitive were the houses built of sods. They were restricted to the bogland areas where other materials were sparse. Sods were generally regarded as makeshift material used for workmen's shelters or sheds. But many tenants evicted by their landlords had rarely anywhere else to go and were so poverty stricken that more substantial material was out of the question. The material was weak so the sods were piled up to form a thick wall. A number of flat stones were laid on top of the walls to take the roof timbers. Sometimes clay was used to bind the sods, and, where timber could be found, it was used as a reinforcement. Door and window openings were usually left rough and then trimmed later with a spade or knife.

Clay walling, with a binding of straw, like the cob walling of Devon, was typical in most districts. The material was cheap, easy to obtain, and apart from the heavy labour involved produced quite substantial buildings. A smooth surface was

*Primitve house built of sods near Toome
Bridge, County Antrim, in 1916*

achieved by shaving the walls with spades
or by plastering, while coats of limewash
helped to make it weatherproof. In some
areas door and window openings were cut
out of the solid clay after the walls were
built. In order to protect the walls further
it was necessary for the roof to be built
with a wide overhang at the eaves. Flat
stones were again used to carry supporting timbers on the clay wall.

Dry-stone walling was used to build
houses in many parts of Ireland. This
was a fairly traditional form of building
dating back to the early Christian

clochain and oratories, but the best
material of all for those who could afford
it was mortar and stone. Lintels to doors
and windows were usually made of
timber but where large stones were
available they were used for lintels.

Roofs were steeply pitched. In East
Ulster roof rafters were carried on large
purlins which span between the gable
walls and cross walls, but elsewhere the
lighter coupled rafters with a collar were
more common. Most were covered with
strips of sod laid straight onto the roof
timbers. The finish was usually a thatch of

straw or heather. In County Down straw was laid in specially-prepared bundles and the thatch plastered down at the eaves, gable and ridge with clay or mud. Along the Atlantic coast the thatch was secured by ropes tied to stone weights or, as along the Antrim coast, with ropes pegged to the wall tops. But over most of the country thatch was secured by twigs to the sod underneath.

Many houses, particularly in North Armagh in the late eighteenth century,

A house at Dingle, County Kerry with the thatch roof roped to secure it

Plan of a one-roomed labourer's cabin near Newcastle West, County Limerick.

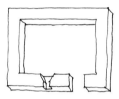

In this house at Teelin, County Donegal, the thatch roof is roped down and then pegged along the eaves and gable end

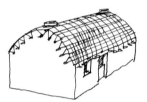

A nineteenth-century house in Antrim

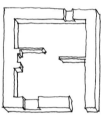

Scollop thatch on a house in County Galway. The thatching round the chimney is similar in detail to some of the black houses on Skye.

One-roomed dwelling, Inishowen, County Mayo, early twentieth century

A weaver's dwelling built about 1850 in Ballydugan townland, County Down

were adapted to meet the changing economy as domestic linen manufacture began to replace small-scale farming. A typical feature of the old weavers' cottages is the outshut built to take a loom. By the late eighteenth century the weaving industry expanded and in some cases a separate loom shop was added forming a three-bay, or in southwest Lough Neagh, a four-bay house. But by the late nineteenth century domestic linen manufacture began to decline.

Larger two-storey houses were generally rebuilt along more fashionable lines or remodelled during the eighteenth century. Thatch was replaced by slate, a trend which continued into the early twentieth century, but for the humbler dwellings such changes occur mainly in this century when thatch has given way to corrugated iron or the asbestos tile.

The poverty of accommodation and general misery of the labouring poor was due, among other things, to exploitation, indifference and mismanagement. Some eighteenth- and nineteenth-century landlords did replan their tenants' housing. Some created whole villages, usually aping some distant Utopia. Bagenalstown (Muine Bheag in County Carlow) was to have been called Versailles while another, Moy, in County Tyrone, was built around a long narrow square and laid out on the plan of Marengo in Lombardy. But most adopted the traditional materials and house plans of the area. Eighteenth-century liberals and colonialists believed that the one way of improving the Irish was to bring them into contact with the civilizing influence of planned and ordered settlements. The nineteenth-century landlords appear to have followed suit, but the Irish, by tradition, were free in spirit if not in reality and these model villages were, if anything, more like a straitjacket than some liberating Utopia.

Places of Interest to Visit

Readers may be interested to visit further places of interest where examples of cottage building, and early industrial and rural life can be seen. The County Museums throughout Britain and Ireland have exhibits illustrating the pattern of local life but the following is a selective list of folk museums and open-air museums that may be of particular interest.

THE WEST COUNTRY
Avon: Blaise Castle House and Hamlet, Henbury, Bristol
Cornwall: Wayside Cottage Folk Museum, Zennor, St Ives
Devon: Museum of Industrial Archaeology, Morwellham Quay, Tamar Valley
Dorset: Milton Abbas, near Blandford Forum
Somerset: Glastonbury Lake Village Museum, High Street, Glastonbury
Wookey Hole Caves and Mill, near Wells

THE SOUTHERN COUNTIES
Berkshire: Museum of English Rural Life, The University, Whiteknights Park, Reading
Buckinghamshire: Milton's Cottage, Chalfont St Giles
Hampshire: Butser Hill Ancient Farm Project, near Petersfield
Wiltshire: Lacock Abbey and Village, Lacock

LONDON'S COUNTRY AND COAST
Essex: Paycocke's House, Coggeshall
Hertfordshire: The Ashwell Village Museum, Ashwell, Baldock
Kent: Smallhythe Place, Smallhythe, near Tenterden (Dame Ellen Terry's house)
London: Geffrye Museum, Kingsland Road, Shoreditch, E.2
London Museum, Barbican, 150 London Wall, E.C.2
Surrey: Guildford Museum, Quarry Street, Guildford
West Sussex: Parsonage Row Cottages, West Tarring
Weald and Downland Open Air Museum, Singleton, Chichester

EAST ANGLIA AND THE FENS
Cambridgeshire: Cambridge and County Folk Museum, 2–3 Castle Street, Cambridge
Norfolk: Iceni Village and Museum, Cockley Cley
Suffolk: The Abbot's Hall Museum of East Anglian Life, Stowmarket

WALES
Gwent: Rural Crafts Museum, Llanvapley, near Abergavenny
Gwynedd: Portmeirion, Cardigan Bay
South Glamorgan: Welsh Folk Museum, St Fagans

THE MIDLANDS
Derbyshire: The Old House Museum, Cunningham Place, Bakewell
Hereford and Worcester: Avoncroft Museum, Stoke Heath, Bromsgrove, Worcester
Black Country Museum (in the Central Museum and Art Gallery), St James's Road, Dudley
Northamptonshire: The Waterways Museum, Stoke Bruerne, Towcester
Salop: Blists Open Air Museum, Telford
Warwickshire: Mary Arden's House, Wilmcote
Anne Hathaway's Cottage, Shottery
West Midlands: Folk Museum, Sarehole Mill, Hall Green, Birmingham

THE INDUSTRIAL NORTH AND THE MOORS
Isle of Man: Manx Village Folk Museum, Cregneash
Lancashire: The Ashworth Museum, Turton Tower, Chapletown Road, Turton
South Yorkshire: Abbeydale Industrial Hamlet, Abbeydale Road South, Sheffield

West Yorkshire: Abbey House Museum, Kirkstall
Folk Museum of West Yorkshire, Shibden Hall, Shibden, Halifax

NORTHUMBERLAND AND THE LAKES
Durham: North of England Open Air Museum, Beamish, near Stanley
North Yorkshire: Ryedale Folk Museum, Hutton-le-Hole
York Castle Museum, Tower Street, York

SCOTLAND
Highland Region: The Highland Folk Museum, Kingussie, Inverness
Strathclyde Region: Open Air Museum, Auchindrain, Argyll
Weaver's Cottage, The Cross, Kilbarchan, Renfrew
Tayside Region: Angus Folk Museum, Kirkwynd, Glamis, Angus

IRELAND
Ulster Folk and Transport Museum, Cultra Manor, Holywood, County Down

A list of *Museums and Galleries in Great Britain and Ireland* is published annually by ABC Travel Guides Ltd of Oldhill, London Road, Dunstable, LU6 3EB, Bedfordshire

Glossary

aisled hall: An open hall with arcaded aisle/s
ashlar: Finely-cut stone laid with close joints
attic: Habitable room within the roof
baffle entry: External entrance planned opposite the side wall of a chimney stack
bally: Group of houses, hamlet
barge board: Board, often carved, fixed to front of gable roof
barmkin: Tower
bastle: Fortified house with animals on ground floor
booley: Shelter for cattle and herdsmen. Irish term
box frame: Timber-frame construction carrying the roof trusses
brace: Diagonal timber strengthening framework
bressumer: Beam directly supporting wall above
brick nogging: Brickwork used to fill the panels of timber-framed buildings
broaches: Pointed rod of wood or iron
buttery: Storage room, usually for drink
byre: Stable for cows
catilide roof: Uninterrupted extension of main roof over outshut
cell: A room
clachan: Hamlet
cob: Mixture of chalk and gravel for walling
coit: *See* laithe house
collar: Horizontal timber tieing together a pair of rafters
corbel: Projecting stone or timber as support
couple: Pair of rafters
crucks: Pair of curved timbers for roof structure
dene: Small wooded valley with a stream
dressings: Careful choice of stone and brickwork
dry-stone walling: Stone laid without mortar
field house: Isolated byre
gable: Vertical wall ending a roof
hafod: Welsh name for a summer dwelling or shieling
hall: Principal room of medieval house
heck: Low internal wall
hipped roof: Roof with sloping ends
inglenook: Area under large chimney
jamb: An upright forming side of door or window opening
jetty: Projection of upper storey
laithe: Building combining barn and byre
laithe house: House, barn and byre under one roof

light: Vertical opening of a window
lintel: Timber or stone bridging an opening
loft: Roof space used for storing
longhouse: Byre and house in one range separated by a through passage
mansard: A roof with two angles of slope on each side
mud and stud: Timber wall of staves plastered with mud
mullion: Upright dividing a window into lights
oriel: Projecting window
outshut: Extension under a lean-to roof
pantile: Curved roofing tile
pargeting: Decorative plasterwork of raised ornamental figures
parlour: Private room
plinth: Projecting base of wall
purlin: Longitudinal timber support for roof carried on walls or roof trusses
quoins: Prepared stonework or brickwork at corners of a building
rail: Horizontal timber in timber-frame wall
reveals: The side of an opening
ridge: Horizontal timber at apex of roof
scarf: Interlocking timber joint
shieling: Hut or roughly-constructed cottage in the uplands for shepherds
shippon: Shed for livestock
sill: Lower horizontal member of window or door frame
soffit: The underside of an arch, beam, etc.
solar: The principal chamber in a medieval house
spar: Timber or metal pole
tie: The main horizontal timber of a roof truss
timber frame: The structural frame of wall or building
tourelle: A small tower
tracery: Ornamental work in a window, screen or panel
voussoir: Tapering or wedge-shaped pieces forming an arch or vault
wattle and daub: Wall filling of twigs or wattles covered with clay
weatherboarding: Horizontal overlapping wooden cladding used to protect timber-framed buildings
witchert: Buckinghamshire term for cob walling

Bibliography

Shell Publications

ARNOLD, JAMES. *The Shell Book of Country Crafts.* John Baker 1968. Revised edition 1977

BOUMFREY, GEOFFREY, Editor. *The Shell Guide to Britain.* Ebury Press and George Rainbird 1964. Second edition 1969

HADFIELD, JOHN, Editor. *The Shell Guide to England.* Michael Joseph and George Rainbird 1970

KILLANIN, Lord and DUIGNAN, MICHAEL V. *The Shell Guide to Ireland.* Ebury Press and George Rainbird 1962. Second edition 1967

MACNIE, DONALD LAMOND and MCLAREN, MORAY. *The New Shell Guide to Scotland.* Ebury Press and George Rainbird 1977

VAUGHAN-THOMAS, WYNFORD and LLEWELLYN, ALUN. *The Shell Guide to Wales.* Michael Joseph and George Rainbird 1969

General Titles

ASHLEY, MAURICE. *England in the Seventeenth Century.* Penguin 1967

BARLEY, M. W. *The English Farmhouse and Cottage.* Routledge & Kegan Paul 1972. *The House and Home.* Studio Vista 1965

BATSFORD, H. and FRY, C. *The English Cottage.* B. T. Batsford 1938

BINDOFF, S. T. *Tudor England.* Penguin 1975

BOUCH, C. M. L. and JONES, G. P. *The Lake Counties 1500–1830.* Manchester University Press 1961

BOWYER, J. *History of Building.* Crosby, Lockwood Staples 1973

BRAUN, HUGH. *Old English Houses.* Faber & Faber 1962

BRIGGS, ASA. *Victorian Cities.* Penguin 1968

BRUNSKILL, R. W. *Illustrated Handbook of Vernacular Architecture.* Faber & Faber 1970. *Vernacular Architecture of the Lake District.* Faber & Faber 1974

BURTON, ANTHONY. *The Canal Builders.* Eyre Methuen 1972

CHAMBERS, J. D. and MINGAY, G. E. *The Agricultural Revolution 1750–1880.* B. T. Batsford 1975

CLIFTON-TAYLOR, ALEC. *The Pattern of English Building.* Faber & Faber 1972

COBBETT, WILLIAM. *Rural Rides* Vols. 1 and 2. J. M. Dent & Son 1966

DANACHAIR, C. Ó *Folk and Farms.* Royal Society of Antiquaries of Ireland 1976

DARLEY, GILLIAN. *Villages of Vision.* The Architectural Press 1975

DUNBAR, J. G. *The Historic Architecture of Scotland.* B. T. Batsford 1966

ELTON, G. R. *England Under the Tudors.* Methuen 1955

EVANS, ESTYN. *Irish Folk Ways.* Routledge & Kegan Paul 1957

GUERNSEY SOCIETY, THE. *The Guernsey Farmhouse.* 1963

H.M.S.O.: Inventories of the Ancient and Historical Monuments of: *Argyll Volume 1 – Kintyre.* 1971. *Argyll Volume 2 – Lorn.* 1975. *The County of Roxburgh* Volumes 1 and 2. 1956. *Selkirk.* 1957. *Stirlingshire* Volume 1. 1963

HOSKINS, W. G. *The Making of the English Landscape.* Penguin 1975

HUDSON, KENNETH. *The Archaeology of Industry.* The Bodley Head 1976

HYAMS, EDWARD. *English Cottage Gardens.* Thomas Nelson & Sons 1970

JONES, S. R. *English Village Homes.* B. T. Batsford 1936

MARSHALL, J. P. *Old Lakeland.* David & Charles 1971

MERCER, ERIC. *English Vernacular Houses.* H.M.S.O. 1975

OLIVER, BASIL. *The Cottages of England.* B. T. Batsford 1929

PLUMB, J. H. *England in the Eighteenth Century.* Penguin 1975

RAMM, H. G., McDOWALL, R. W. and MERCER, ERIC. *Shielings and Bastles.* H.M.S.O. 1970

SINCLAIR, COLIN. *Thatched Houses of the Old Highlands.* Oliver & Boyd 1953

SMITH, P. *Houses of the Welsh Countryside.* H.M.S.O. 1975

STEVENS, JOAN. *Old Jersey Houses.* Five Oaks Press 1965

TATE, W. E. *The English Village Community.* Victor Gollancz 1967

THOMPSON, E. P. *The Making of the English Working Class.* Penguin 1975

THOMSON, DAVID. *England in the Nineteenth Century.* Penguin 1975. *England in the Twentieth Century.* Penguin 1976

TRENT, CHRISTOPHER. *England in Brick and Stone.* Anthony Blond 1958

TREVELYAN, G. M. *English Social History.* Penguin 1974

TRUEMAN, A. *Geology and Scenery in England and Wales.* Penguin 1971

WEST, TRUDY. *The Timber-frame House in England.* David & Charles 1971

WOODFORDE, JOHN. *The Truth about Cottages.* Routledge & Kegan Paul 1969

ULSTER FOLKLIFE.Published by The Ulster Folk and Transport Museum. Volume 2, 1956 DANACHAIR. C. Ó *Three House Types.* MCCOURT, D. *The Outshut House-type and Its Distribution in County Londonderry.* Volume 8, 1962 – GAILEY, A. *Two Cruck Houses near Lurgan.* MCCOURT, D. *Weavers' Houses around South-west Lough Neagh.* Volumes 15 and 16, 1970 – MCCOURT, D. *The House with Bedroom over Byre: a long-house derivative.* Volume 22, 1976 – GAILEY, A. *The Housing of the Rural Poor in Nineteenth-Century Ulster*

Illustration Acknowledgments

The producers of this book would like to thank all those who have given permission for pictures to be reproduced here. The drawings have been specially drawn by the author but where they have been adapted from previous work these are listed below.

Aerofilms Limited   117, 181 (below)
Architectural Review (Photo: Sam Lambert) 133
Professor M. W. Barley   71 (above), 89, 90, 99, 100 (above left), 111 (right), 113, 127, 130 (right), 131 (middle), 152, 154, 162, 166 (left), 167, 178, 179 (above), 180, 190, 194 (below right), 213
British Tourist Authority   jacket, title page
Dr R. W. Brunskill   24, 26 (above left), 36 (below), 38 (right), 39 (below), 40 (left), 43 (right), 44 (right), 46 (left), 50
Cadbury Collection, Birmingham Public Libraries, Local Studies   156
G. L. Carlisle   224–5
Crown Copyright:
The National Monuments Record, England 37, 44, 45, 84–5, 101 (below), 147, 149, 153, 155, 163, 164, 174, 175, 176, 181 (above)
The Controller, Her Majesty's Stationery Office: (Photos: Royal Commission on Ancient and Historical Monuments in Wales)   33, 139, 141 (above), 143;
Illustrations based on drawings from *English Vernacular Houses* by Eric Mercer 16 (below right), 17 (left), 30 (left), 38 (left), 39 (top right), 43 (left), 49, 112 (below), 166 (above left); from *Houses of the Welsh Countryside* by Peter Smith   134, 136, 137, 138, 140; and from *Argyll – An Inventory of the Ancient Monuments*   186 (below), 198 (left), 199

Gillian Darley   82, 94, 101 (above), 118, 119, 120–1, 132, 182
David A. Gowans   216–17, 222–3
Edwin Gunn   52 (below)
A. F. Kersting   200–1
The Mansell Collection   21, 60, 64, 72–3, 203, 219
Reproduced by courtesy of the Trustees, The National Gallery, London   12
The Radio Times Hulton Picture Library   19, 69, 87, 141 (below), 157, 165, 169
Royal Commission on Ancient Monuments, Scotland   187, 188–9, 192, 193, 195, 196–7, 214–15
British Architectural Library, The Royal Institute of British Architects, London   79, 108
Kenneth Scowen   42, 65, 88, 95, 96, 115, 124–5, 126, 144–5, 151, 183, 206, 207, 210–11, 220–1, 230–1, 235, 236
Colin Sinclair   220, 226 (below), 227
Edwin Smith   27, 28, 48, 55, 61, 66, 78, 81, 93, 97, 103, 105, 107, 109, 115, 128, 129, 130, 158–9, 171
James Stirling   83
W. Gwyn Thomas   140
The Ulster Folk and Transport Museum 233 (above), 234, 238 (above), 239, 240, 241, 242, 243
Yorkshire Post Newspapers, Leeds   168

Index